Anth

CW00420540

Lent
for the not-so-holy

the columba press

First published in 2006 by
the columba press
55A Spruce Avenue, Stillorgan Industrial Park,
Blackrock, Co Dublin

Cover by Bill Bolger
Origination by The Columba Press
Printed in Ireland by ColourBooks Ltd, Dublin

ISBN 978 1 85607 546 6

Acknowledgements
Biblical quotations are taken from the *New Revised Standard Version*,
copyright © 1989, by the Division of Christian Education of the
National Council of the Churches of Christ in the United States of
America. Used by permission.

Contents

Foreword

The season of Lent is a kind of journey, a pilgrimage perhaps, with the promise of something glorious at the end. The readings used at the Roman Catholic Mass on the forty-six days which include Holy Week, are a guide for us, the pilgrims, and this book is an attempt, often based on those readings, to point the way, to illuminate the journey for people like myself.

I am not holy; nor am I a scholar or a theologian, but someone who would like to make a good Lent and to share this walk of faith with others, encouraging them, I hope, to discover their own insights and inspiration, as they face their struggles and doubts and are consoled and uplifted by the Holy Spirit. I hope above all that each of us can deepen our love of Jesus Christ, whose terrible journey this was.

Introduction

This book is in no way prescriptive. If we imagine the journey it takes us as leading us from the beginning (Ash Wednesday) to the end (Holy Saturday), there will be all sorts of things to discover, listen to, imagine, explore and respond to along the way. My own journey focuses on only a few of the incidents and people that happened to strike me particularly at a certain moment. For instance I dwelt for some time on the rather mysterious figure of Simon of Cyrene, and the fate of Judas led me to consider the implications of suicide. Different readers will be led to pursue other paths, and some may like to write their own reflections.

We might ask, what should we do when embarking on such a journey? We could begin with prayer, asking God not only to accompany us but to strengthen and inspire us on the way. It is good to travel light: if we have the Sunday Missal and the Weekday Missal, it will be easier to refer to the readings, but we can always look them up in our Bible. Pen and paper are useful too, for jotting down notes or writing reflections.

Clearly, we will need to set aside some time each day, and it will be helpful if we can follow the text day by day, so that we are reading and thinking about the Fourth Sunday of Lent, for example, on the Fourth Sunday in Lent!

Sometimes it feels appropriate to pause at certain places in the text, to have a time of reflection on what has just gone before. This is not the sort of book to run through at speed; the readers should feel free to take their time and pause to reflect when this feels right.

Ash Wednesday
Joel 2:12-18; Matthew 6:1-6, 16-18

It seems to me that there is no better way to begin a Lenten journey than by reading and taking to heart George Herbert's poem, *Love (iii)*.

> Love bade me welcome: yet my soul drew back,
>> Guiltie of dust and sinne.
> But quick-eyed Love, observing me grow slack
>> From my first entrance in,
> Drew nearer to me, sweetly questioning,
>> If I lack'd anything.
>
> A guest, I answer'd, worthy to be here:
>> Love said, You shall be he.
> I the unkinde, ungrateful? Ah, my deare,
>> I cannot look on thee.
> Love took my hand, and smiling did reply,
>> Who made the eyes but I?
>
> Truth Lord, but I have marr'd them: let my shame
>> Go where it doth deserve.
> And know you not, sayes Love, who bore the blame?
>> My deare, then I will serve.
> You must sit down, sayes Love, and taste my meat:
>> So I did sit and eat.

Don't we all feel unworthy? And isn't God's love great enough to forgive and bless us all?

This is the first day of our Lent. Perhaps we need to ask ourselves some questions before we begin. Why do I want to succeed in 'making' a good Lent? Is it because I am hoping to save my soul, and get to heaven? Is it because I want to widen my understanding of Jesus and deepen my love for him? Or is it because I want to become someone who looks outward to the needs of my neighbours and of the world and takes seriously Christ's command that we should love one another?

If our fundamental purpose is to love God and our brothers and sisters more, then we can leave the saving of our souls where it belongs, to him. Sometimes people have the mistaken idea of what it means to be holy. It certainly does not mean being self-obsessed and only concerned about keeping the rules. Rather, I suggest, it means responding to God by becoming the person he wants us to be.

So, having answered the question, why do I want to make a good Lent, we now ask ourselves how, and in particular on this first day, what sort of things should I be doing, or planning to do?

If we have the time and opportunity, it's very helpful to read the scriptures of each day, using the Weekday and Sunday Missals. In case this is not possible the Bible references for each day will be at the top of the page at the beginning of the day. If you are following this book, you will need to take a little time each day not just to read it but to think about it, and perhaps choose one or two passages to reflect on at some length, such as the Herbert poem.

Traditionally, Lent has been a time for giving up: cigarettes, or chocolate or alcohol (there can be mixed motives here!), giving up going to the theatre or the cinema or the pub, doing without something we especially enjoy. We can also fast, and some people stoically spend hours each day without food. And we can give alms, supporting whatever charity appeals to us. It seems particularly appropriate to do without some food, and give the money we save towards alleviating hunger in the poorest countries.

For myself, I do like to make a resolution on Ash Wednesday, and even more I like to keep it faithfully till Easter Day. But I have to question some of the more usual commitments. I don't believe that God wants us to make ourselves ill by fasting, and I wonder if it isn't more helpful when rather than giving up something, we take something on. It might be writing to a prisoner on Death Row (a commitment which would clearly have to last beyond Lent); it might be visiting someone in hospital or praying regularly for someone who annoys us. It could be even as simple as making sure we smile at everyone we meet.

The advantage of this kind of resolution is that it makes a positive contribution to someone's life. My doing without chocolate is of no use to anyone else.

Another thought about Lent is this: in the northern hemisphere, the season coincides with the burgeoning of spring. In the country, and in the parks and gardens of our towns, we can watch the unfolding of beauty as one by one the different flowers come into bloom, birds break into song and build their nests, lambs frolic and trees burst into new leaf, all transforming the dark dull world of winter, all vibrant with the promise of new life. One way to observe Lent is to enjoy the beauty of creation and lift our minds to God in thanksgiving and praise for the gift of new life.

It is also traditional for Christians, especially Roman Catholics, to 'do' the Stations of the Cross in Lent. This is certainly an effective way of concentrating our minds on Christ's suffering, but it is most helpful when the words, and indeed the choice of Stations, are such that they really touch a chord for the person following them. It suits some of us to pray the Stations in church, in the company of others, but other people prefer to pray them at home, alone and in their own time. Nowadays there are many books available which guide us along the Way of the Cross. Better still, perhaps, is making up the Stations ourselves. This is not as daunting as it sounds: even a single word, such as 'pity' or 'anger', can speak to us as we meditate on the different stages of Christ's journey to Calvary.

It is a pity that many people cannot get to Mass or a church service on Ash Wednesday. First of all, as with the Veneration of the Cross on Good Friday, we have a sense of solidarity, as everyone in the church forms a procession of people going up to receive the ashes. Secondly, there is a kind of solemn intimacy when the celebrant makes a cross of ashes on our foreheads. If at the same time he says:

'Remember, man (woman) you are dust
and to dust you will return,'
I find the moment sobering and humbling. Yet at the same time, something in me rebels, and I think, No! I am more than dust! I am made in the image of God, his daughter, and he wants me to have life to the full!

However, there is an alternative admonition:
'Turn away from sin and be faithful to the gospel.'
I think I am more compliant if these words are said to me. 'Turn away from sin'. Surely a good way to begin our Lent but quite a tall order for some of us who are not-so-holy. Turning away from sin is for most of us, alas, the process of a lifetime, hardly something that can be accomplished in a day, or even the six weeks of Lent. But the readings of Ash Wednesday are consoling:
'Yet even now,' says the Lord,
'return to me with all your heart,
with fasting, with weeping, and with mourning;
rend your hearts and not your clothing.
Return to the Lord, your God,
for he is gracious and merciful,
slow to anger and abounding in steadfast love,
and relents from punishing.'
Joel 2:12,13

Now let us pray:
Dear Loving Father,
I come before you at the beginning of this Lent, and I ask that your Holy Spirit will enlighten and guide me through the days. You know all about me: you know my sins, my disappointments, my weaknesses, my fears, my failures and my successes. I am sorry for everything wrong that I have done, and I resolve today to turn away from sin and be converted to a new way of living. Give me the courage to change, and to stay with you, Lord.

You know me just as I am, yet you not only accept me but love me. Help me this Lent to find new ways of following

13

Jesus Christ and of serving my sisters and brothers. I praise and thank you from a full heart. Amen.

Most of us find it hard to believe that God truly loves us just as we are, especially as he, more than anyone, knows what we are really like, even in our innermost thoughts. I am always moved by Charles Wesley's account of his meeting with a prisoner, who was so astounded at this good news.

Wesley went to Newgate Prison to preach to the condemned prisoners, and visited one of them in his cell, 'a poor black that had robbed his master. I told him of One who came down from heaven to save lost sinners and him in particular ... He listened with all the signs of eager astonishment, the tears trickled down his cheeks while he cried, 'What! Was it for me? Did God suffer all this for so poor a creature as me?'

'I left him waiting for salvation.'

If you are not too tired at the end of the day, you may like to reflect for a few moments, perhaps with a lighted candle, on these words from Psalm 139:

O Lord you have searched me and known me.
You know when I sit down and when I rise up;
You discern my thoughts from far away.
You search out my path and my lying down
And are acquainted with all my ways.
Even before a word is on my tongue,
O Lord, you know it completely.
Psalm 139:1-4

For personal thought or group discussion:
1. How do you feel at the end of this day?
2. You may like to write your own prayer as Lent begins.

Thursday after Ash Wednesday
Deuteronomy 30:15-20; Luke 9:22-25

Today's readings are about choice:

Moses said to the people ... 'I have set before you life and death, blessings and curses. Choose life, so that you and your descendants may live, loving the Lord your God, obeying him, for that means life to you.

Deuteronomy 30:19,20

The sophisticated life of people of the twenty-first century in western culture is very different from life in the time of Moses, but the message 'Choose life', still holds good today. For us this choice means living with God as our centre, trusting in him, walking in his ways. We have the teachings of Jesus, the values of the gospel as our guide. And choosing life does not just mean obeying the rules, it means embracing whatever circumstances we encounter with courage and generosity. It means living life to the full.

Today's second reading is taken from Luke's gospel:

If any want to become my followers, let them deny themselves and take up their cross daily and follow me.

Luke 9:23

There are some misunderstandings about these words of Jesus. We often hear people say, with a rueful grin, of their arthritic knee or their crotchety neighbour, 'Oh well, it's my cross: I'll just have to bear it!' When Jesus asked people to take up their cross, he didn't mean, 'Put up with what has befallen you,' he meant 'Choose to put yourself last', and sometimes, 'Choose to suffer.'

Some people, interpreting his words in this way, imagine that they are not really true followers of Jesus unless they can match up to heroes and saints like Oscar Romero, Maximilian Kolbe, Edith Stein and Dietrich Bonhoeffer, who sacrificed their lives for love of God and love of humanity. They were wonderful people, but only very few of us are likely to find ourselves in a position to choose whether to carry our cross to the extreme of giving our lives.

However, this does not mean that we are exempt from the requirement to carry our cross daily. It will mostly consist of something very ordinary: simply our willingness to sacrifice our own wishes for the sake of someone else in the course of our everyday lives.

On a cold winter's night, I can choose whether to stay at home by the fire or go out to visit a bereaved friend. If I go out, I am carrying my cross, albeit a very little one. Taking up my cross and following Jesus means being selfless rather than selfish, denying our own wishes for the sake of another. It is the way of Christ, the way of love. He was literally to carry his cross; as his disciples we try to shoulder whatever burdens we have freely chosen, be they great or small, with cheerfulness and generosity.

So let us choose wisely, and choose life!

Today's psalm begins by praising the good and holy:
They are like trees
planted by streams of water,
which yield their fruit in its season
and their leaves do not wither.
Psalm 1:3

This is a lovely image, but not one that applies to me. I see myself more as a plant struggling to reach the light. And the older I get the more I realise how alike most of us are. There are so many superficial differences in both appearance and behaviour, but our fears and hopes, our lack of confidence, our sense of unworthiness are common to nearly all of us. My image of myself as a plant struggling to reach the light was spontaneous, but I guess that nearly everyone I know would identify with it or with a similar image of themselves.

Yet I am certain that this is not what Jesus wants us to be. He said, 'I came that they may have life, and have it abundantly' (John 10:10) and St Irenaeus said, 'The greatest glory of God is a human being fully alive.' So my picture of that pathetic little plant won't do. God wants me, and all of us, to grow in wisdom and holiness, to be fully alive, the friends in whom his joy is complete.

For personal thought or group discussion:
What is your cross?
Can you think of an image to describe yourself?

Friday after Ash Wednesday
Isaiah 58:1-9; Matthew 9:14-15

Today's reading from Isaiah could be a sort of Mission Statement for the whole of Lent. I find it one of the most powerful passages in the Old Testament.

> Is not this the fast that I choose:
> to loose the bonds of injustice,
> to undo the thongs of the yoke,
> to let the oppressed go free,
> and to break every yoke?
> Is it not to share your bread with the hungry,
> and bring the homeless poor into your house:
> when you see them naked, to cover them,
> and not to hide yourself from your own kin?
> Then your light shall break forth like the dawn,
> and your hurts be quickly healed.
> *Isaiah 58:6-8*

I do not for a moment want to suggest that there is no point in fasting: it is practised by most, if not all, the great religions, and the experience often gives people a purer focus on the things of God. What the writer of this passage is trying to get across to the Jews is, I think, that God is not so much concerned with how well we practise our devotions, as he is with the way we treat one another. We are more truly holy when justice, rather than correct religious practice, is our priority. The figure of Jesus on his cross is not a model of piety; he is an object of wretched humiliation. But his arms are outstretched as though to embrace us all. When I fast and recite prayers, it is as if I am aiming to reach up to God, to establish an unbreakable bond between God and me, me and God. But when I make it my purpose to heal, protect, rescue, serve and struggle on behalf of my fellowmen and women, then God is my companion.

Reading these lines from Isaiah we may feel that God is asking not less than everything. When I go through the passage line by line and challenge myself, I feel disheartened and ashamed. I can't live up to this. It's true that I make an effort: I would gladly give food to someone who is hungry; I do give quite a lot of my clothes to asylum seekers who have virtually none; I do become politically involved in urging my member of parliament to act justly and persuade others to do so ... but when I look at these lines: 'bring the homeless poor into your house', I just can't bring myself to say Yes. I have plenty of excuses: I have only one spare room which I keep for my family and friends. I couldn't take a complete stranger into my house – could I? He might be on drugs, a thief, or worse ...

Late one night there was a knock on Estelle's door. On the doorstep stood a thin youth she had never seen before. He was about seventeen years old, had a shaven head and was wearing a grubby sleeveless shirt.

'I'm sorry to trouble you, Miss,' he said, 'but I've only just arrived here and I can't find nowhere to sleep. I tried the Shelter but it's full, and the lady said you might have a bed.'

Estelle hesitated. It was a bitterly cold night and he was shivering. He seemed harmless enough. But she was alone, and she was scared.

'Look,' she said, 'I'm sorry but I can't put you up.'

'Please,' he begged, 'it will only be for one night.'

Estelle hesitated again. She could at least invite him in for a minute, out of the cold. But she remembered the stories she'd heard ...

'I'm really sorry,' she said. 'Look – are you hungry?' He nodded so she told him to wait. She left him on the doorstep while she hurriedly made two thick sandwiches and added a chocolate bar. Half-way back to the door she had a thought. She ran upstairs and grabbed a blanket from the airing cupboard.

But when she got back to the door the boy had gone. Estelle shrugged. He can't have been all that hungry, she thought. But when she went up to bed that night and switched on the electric blanket before slipping under her warm duvet, she thought of him somewhere out there on the streets. If he gets hypothermia and dies, this will be my fault, she told herself. She couldn't get to sleep.

But next day Estelle met the boy again. She probably wouldn't have recognised him but he smiled and said 'Hi!' He was wearing a thick coat, gloves and woolly hat.

'Did you find somewhere to sleep?' she asked.

'Yes – no – well, somebody found me' he said. 'Mrs Jenkins, Kath. Do you know her?'

Estelle did. She was a funny little woman, who lived alone too. Estelle had sometimes wondered if she was quite right in the head. She always looked shabby and a bit un-kempt.

The boy noticed her puzzled expression. 'She goes out when it's really cold,' he said, 'just in case there's somebody like me with nowhere to go. She hasn't got much, but she made me some soup and I had a bath and she washed my clothes and let me sleep in her bed. She slept on the sofa: she says she likes it. She's all right.'

Estelle didn't know what to say. In the end she managed, 'Good luck!' Then she went home, feeling ashamed and wishing she could be like 'Little Mrs Jenkins'.

Of course, none of us is perfect. It's good to recognise this, and it's good to know ourselves and see our failings clearly. I have to admit that I am not as generous and compassionate and accept-ing of others as I would like to be, as God wants me to be. I have to believe that with his help I can change and grow.

For personal thought or group discussion:
How does Isaiah's challenge strike you?

Saturday after Ash Wednesday
Isaiah 58:9-14; Luke 5:27-32

Today's first reading follows on from yesterday's. Isaiah's imagery is beautiful, and God's promise to those who work for justice is inspiring, but it makes very sad reading, because from it we realise that the two greatest obstacles to the establishment of fairness in the world today, namely war and hunger, are the same enemies of right thinking and right action as prevailed so long ago in the time of Isaiah. Indeed, we supposedly civilised people have made the earth an even less happy place. Our sophisticated weaponry is maiming and killing the innocent, men women and children in nearly every country; the gap between the rich and poor grows wider every day. When will we ever learn?

If we listen to Isaiah, and think about the meaning of his words, then surely we must act. 'Blessed are they who hunger and thirst for righteousness,' said Jesus. In scripture the same word is sometimes translated as righteousness and sometimes justice. If we want to follow Jesus, and to be like him, then we are called to join the struggle for justice, and not to give up even when it seems that things will never change. *We* can change: from lukewarm to deeply committed Christians, from resigned, apathetic individuals who have long given up hope of making a difference, to people who believe they can do just that.

It is tempting, of course, to do nothing, to ask, what can one person possibly hope to do against such odds? I like the story of the sparrow which lay on its back in the gutter with its thin little legs pointing upwards. 'What on earth are you doing?' asked a passer-by. 'Well,' said the sparrow, 'I heard that the sky is going to fall in today, and one has to do one's bit, doesn't one?'

Isaiah made a wonderful promise to those who were willing to join the struggle for justice:

If you remove the yoke from among you,
the pointing of the finger, the speaking of evil,

21

if you offer your food to the hungry
and satisfy the needs of the afflicted,
then your light shall rise in the darkness
and your gloom be like the noonday.
The Lord will guide you continually,
and satisfy your needs in parched places,
and make your bones strong;
and you shall be like a watered garden,
like a spring of water
whose waters never fail.
Isaiah 58:9-11

I like the idea of my life being like a watered garden, but for people who lived in the time of Isaiah, that image would have been even more potent and wonderful, for the fields of the Middle East were, and are, often parched and thirsty and therefore unable to produce crops, 'like a dry, weary land without water'. For me personally, the image of a watered garden is especially appealing. If I could choose, I would have a stream running through my garden. I would receive so much pleasure from the water-loving plants on its banks like water-forget-me-nots and kingcups to mention only two.

I find the gospel reading today consoling. I admitted to being a sinner as we began our Lenten journey. Already, some of my faults must be only too obvious to the reader. So it's wonderful to read in Luke's gospel:

The Pharisees and their scribes were complaining to his disciples, saying, 'Why do you eat with tax collectors and sinners?' Jesus answered, 'Those who are well have no need of a physician, but those who are sick; I have come to call not the righteous but sinners to repentance.'

We know that Jesus was happy to mix with tax-collectors (greedy extortionists) and prostitutes and counted them among his friends. I hope I may be counted among them too.

Some years ago, a friend of mine, Dermot, a devout Catholic who spent his days working for the Legion of Mary by befriending prostitutes in London, died suddenly. His funeral was held in a big church, but by the time I arrived, thinking I was early, there was standing room only. Several priests con-celebrated the Mass and an eminent clergyman preached, praising Dermot for his holiness. On the coffin lay a single white rose, the gift of a prostitute. As we left the church, a passer-by, seeing the stream of people pouring out of the building, asked 'Was he someone famous?' 'Yes,' I answered, 'he was someone famous,' and silently added, He was fa-mous in the eyes of God, and in the eyes of the streetwalkers who were his friends.

Lost Boy
I dream of a watered garden.
There is a little beck splashing over the stones,
its water sparkling and clear as glass
blue in the spring sunshine.
Primula candelabra, in all their rainbow colours
Grace the bank with elegance,
And lower down, fat yellow kingcups grow.
There is a kingfisher if I can spot him,
And sometimes, dragonflies.
But most of all I like to lie in bed,
my window open to the sky
breathing in the clean, sweet scent of blossom
and listening to the music
of my laughing beck.

I wake from my dream.
There is no watered garden,
only the outline of the high-rise flats above me
and the filth of this back alley.
The smell is suffocationg:
the stink of stale drink, bodies unwashed for weeks,
the stench of human waste.
I get to my feet, disturbing a rat.
I am cold and oh so hungry;
I need to score,
then everything will be all right.
I remember my dream, and wonder,
will someone find me and show me another way?

For personal thought or group discussion:
How did the story of Dermot and the poem 'Lost Boy' make you
feel?

First Sunday of Lent, Year C
Deuteronomy 26:4-10; Romans 10:8-13; Luke 4: 1-13

Sometimes, when we are reading scripture, some words seem to fly off the page and strike us. Often these words turn out to have a spiritual significance for us. But when I began to read the passage from Deuteronomy on this first Sunday of Lent, the words that seemed to hit me between the eyes were not particularly remarkable from a spiritual point of view; they were: 'My father was a wandering Aramean.'

The reason for the strong impression that these words made on me is that I know a wandering Aramean and what is more, he is someone dear to me who has had a powerful effect on my thinking. Salomon is his name. I first met him when he was about twenty. He had come to England from Belgium in order to improve his English. He needed this because he was hoping to become a lawyer so as to defend the rights of his people.

Salomon was a Christian. He was born and grew up in a small mountain village in the back of beyond between the Tigris and the Euphrates. In his village, Zaz, everyone was a Christian. Nobody except the priest could read or write. There was no doctor, no school. When Salomon was about five years old he was sent up into the high pastures with a gun to protect the sheep from wolves. Then one day the life of Zaz was turned upside down. The Kurds arrived in great numbers and demanded that the village convert to Islam. Rather than do this, the people fled. They were refugees with nowhere to go. Eventually they were put on planes and taken to Belgium. Salomon told us, 'In four hours my mother had to travel through four centuries.'

By the time we met Salomon he had learnt to read and write and spoke French very well. One evening he came to our home with some other young people, and someone asked him if he would recite the Our Father in Aramaic, the language of Jesus. We all fell silent and prayed with him, as he spoke the words. It was a powerful moment.

Later, when we visited him in Liège, we reminded Salomon of this occasion, and shortly afterwards he brought us a scroll, which is framed and on our bedroom wall, containing the words of the Our Father in Aramaic. But I think what impressed me most about Salomon was his gentle remark, said with no hint of criticism, 'The difference between the English and French and our people, is that for you it's important to have: for us it's important to be.' This seems a perceptive and profound statement on the lips of the boy from Zaz.

Probably because I am very fond of Salomon, and also very ignorant about the politics and religions of the Middle East, I tended to think of the Kurds as 'baddies', or vaguely, the enemy. But then I met Nihat, a young Kurd, a refugee from Turkey who at the time I met him was seeking asylum in Britain. Now I am very fond of Nihat too.

I suppose I have always known that people should never be labelled, categorised, considered to be 'goodies' or 'baddies', but my friendship with these two young men has brought home to me forcefully how wrong it is to make facile judgements not only about people but about races and religions. Salomon and Nihat are two attractive, intelligent young men who have lived through shattering experiences but are both committed to the cause of right. In my much longer life I have never had to suffer as they have, and in the face of this I am very hesitant to be dogmatic or judgemental about anyone. As St Paul tells us in today's second reading, 'Scripture makes no distinction between Jew and Greek: all belong to the same Lord, who is rich enough, however many ask for his help, for everyone who calls on the name of the Lord will be saved.'

Today's gospel describes the temptation of Jesus in the desert. Perhaps it was chosen so that we might give time to reflecting on our own temptations and our sins.

We know that Jesus was like us in all things but sin, and that he became incarnate as a fully human being. I cannot think that, terrible though his temptations in the wilderness were, it was the end of them when he came back from the desert, so that he began his mission and carried it through like some unassailable Superman. I believe that Jesus was like us, that he was often frail and vulnerable, wide-open to all sorts of temptation as we are.

I can imagine that there were times when he was tempted to run away from the constant pressure of the crowds, when he was tempted to lose patience with the disciples, tempted to show more love to some people than others, tempted to give in to fear, tiredness, loneliness, tempted to take a holiday!

For personal thought or group discussion:
Why do you think we sometimes 'label' people?

Monday in the First Week of Lent
Leviticus 19:1-2, 11-18; Matthew 25:31-46

Today's readings, whether heard at Mass or read at home, are enough to make any committed Christian quail or, if quailing doesn't suit their temperament, tear their hair! In the first reading from Leviticus there is a list of things we must do and a much longer list of things we must not do, such as cursing the dumb and putting an obstacle in a blind man's way.

If you are feeling disheartened after this, the gospel may only intimidate you further, because it consists of Christ's dramatic depiction of the Last Judgement when the sheep and the poor goats are separated. I write 'poor' goats because I have always had a soft spot for sheep but was recently enchanted by a flock of goats with their gambolling kids, so that it seems tough on the goats to be identified with the wicked.

My remarks so far today have been somewhat flippant, but of course I do take the whole business of becoming holy seriously. I don't think we can expect to become perfect, but I believe we are all called to grow into the kind of people God wants us to be. As I understand it, holy people are those who are both inward and outward looking, open to the Holy Spirit and to others, with God, not self, as their centre. They may not be perfect, but they are full of enthusiasm, ready to change and grow. They look for God in everything and everyone. Very often they are people wounded by life; always they have the capacity to love.

The Last Judgement is in essence a declaration of what matters to God. It does not mention praying, or going to the synagogue, or reading the scripture, or keeping the law. It is entirely concerned with how we treat our brothers and sisters, in other words, with justice. This is what is important to God; this is the mark of the Christian.

Marilyn had always wanted to be a good Christian. She spent a lot of time in prayer and never missed a church service. She read the bible and spiritual books and attended retreats and quiet days. She visited people in hospital and gave generously to charity. She belonged to a Justice and Peace group and demonstrated and marched for what she believed to be right.

On this day, Monday in the first week of Lent, she listened to the gospel and when she got home she took out her missal again and copied out the description of the Last Judgement. Then she ticked off the good things she did.

She sent money for those who were starving, she did voluntary work at the drop-in centre for refugees, she gave many of her clothes to charity, she visited the sick and (the one that cost her the most) became a prison visitor. When she had ticked all these, Marilyn copied out this sentence in her best handwriting:

Come, you that are blessed by the Father,
inherit the kingdom prepared for you
from the foundation of the world.
Matthew 25:34

She placed the text above her bed.

There were two things that Marilyn may have forgotten: first, it never occurred to her to ask why she did all these good things. Secondly, she didn't remember what Paul wrote to the Corinthians:

If I speak in the tongues of mortals and of angels, but do not have love, I am a noisy gong or a clanging cymbal. And if I have prophetic powers, and understand all mysteries and all knowledge, and if I have all knowledge, and if I have all faith, so as to remove mountains, but do not have love, I am nothing. If I give away all my possessions, and if I hand over my body so that I may boast, but do not have love, I gain nothing.
1 Corinthians 13:1-3

Only God and Marilyn know what the motive for her good works was; only God and Marilyn know whether or not she worked for justice with love.

Tuesday in the First Week of Lent
Isaiah 55:10-11; Matthew 6:7-15

Today's psalm contains a beautiful and consoling message:
The Lord is close to the broken-hearted
and saves the crushed in spirit.
Psalm 33 (34):18

The world is continually beset by devastating disasters: tsunamis, hurricanes, earthquakes, mudslides and floods ... People are constantly beset by overwhelming tragedies: cancer, violence, suicide, starvation, disease ... Christians, people of different faiths, and atheists ask the same question: 'Where is God in all this?' Some misfortune is caused by human actions, through wickedness or less directly through the greed of many men and women seeking money and power. But others are beyond the control of mankind: natural disasters, deformities, so-called acts of God.

We believe that God does not cause suffering. If those who believe he is all-powerful are right, then we have no answer to the question, 'Why doesn't he put an end to suffering?' We simply do not know. Personally I do not believe that God has complete control over everything. I see him as vulnerable, as sharing our weakness, as being with us when our lives are shattered, our hearts broken.

The problem of suffering was brought home to me powerfully when I was teaching physically disabled children in a religious education lesson. Here is a story I wrote at that time:

'I rather like the look of you, Miss,' piped up five-year-old Rory. I suppose I'm as susceptible as anyone to flattery but I guessed this was sincere, even though he had never seen my face, or any face. I think he simply meant 'I like you.'

Rory was born blind. He is one of those feisty children, brimming over with life and high spirits, hypersensitive in all the ways he can be, responsive and alert and fearless as he rides his two-wheeler bicycle over the grass. My heart is in

30

my mouth, but Rory's heart beats steadily under his Newcastle United tee shirt.

The RE syllabus I've drawn up for Rory's class includes the story of the blind man of Jericho, but this year I'm going to drop it. I know only too well how the conversation would go at the end of the story. 'Miss, why doesn't Jesus heal me? I know he loves me, and I love him, so why doesn't he make me able to see?'

'He would, Rory, if only he was here.'

'But he is here. You said he was. He promised he would be with us always. So why …?'

The answer to Rory's question is 'I don't know.' I don't know why we suffer. I don't know why, after we, and everyone we knew had prayed so hard for him to recover, our little son died.

What I do know is that God will not forsake us, that in the very worst times he will be there with us, sharing our grief and pain, because he is close to the broken-hearted.

In today's gospel we hear of the teaching of Jesus on prayer. First, he discourages us from babbling our prayers, 'heaping up empty phrases', and gives us the clear example of the Our Father as a model for prayer. It has certainly stood the test of time, and the more we think about it the more we learn. It is a deceptively simple prayer and is truly profound.

When I read this passage quite a long time ago and saw that Jesus was not happy with the 'babbling of prayers', I thought immediately of the group of women in my church who recite the rosary every day before Mass. Their voices are rather strident and they race through the prayers at an astonishing speed. I was pleased to think that Jesus was 'getting at' them!

But of course he wasn't. I understand now that no-one has any right to judge someone else's way of praying and certainly not to presume that their own way is better. People rattling through the rosary may well be praying fervently at some deeper level, and 'telling our beads' is an ancient tradition in other faiths as well as our own. Sometimes it is a method of aiding concentration; on other occasions it may be a way of entering into the joys and sufferings of Jesus.

Aside from the rosary, prayer is something that happens when someone gives time and space to be alone with God, open to him, listening to him, relaxing in his presence. Words may be spoken or not; it doesn't matter. There are no rules to be kept or broken. The Our Father and the rosary are both valid ways of praying, and prayer is a personal and nourishing encounter with God.

For personal thought or group discussion:
What way of praying are you most comfortable with?

Wednesday in the First Week of Lent
Jonah 3:1-10; Luke 11:29-32

The first two days of this week have been rather heavy and intense, with a great deal to think about, so today we will simply spend the time with Jonah, the likeable, funny, very human prophet. He is mentioned in both the first reading and the gospel today, but his story (a short one!) is not told in full.

It is a pity that the name Jonah has come to have a connotation that is less than cheerful. It means 'bad luck'; a 'Jonah' is someone who spoils things or brings a curse on them, whereas when we get to know him we find there's a lot more to him than that, both bad and good.

The first we hear of Jonah is when God tells him to go to the great city of Nineveh and cry out against them for their wickedness. But Jonah doesn't like the idea of this at all and, unlike the other noble prophets in the Old Testament, rebels against God's instructions and runs away, or tries to.

He goes to Joppa and pays his fare to travel to Tarshish, presumably thinking God won't find him there. But God has other ideas: he causes such a great storm at sea that the ship seems likely to be wrecked. The sailors are very frightened, and throw their cargo overboard, to lighten the vessel.

Meanwhile, Jonah is below decks, fast asleep. The captain wakes him and orders him to call on his God to save them. Then the sailors decide to cast lots to find out who was responsible for this disaster. The lot falls on Jonah and the sailors question him asking who he is. Jonah, who clearly has some courage, replies: 'I am a Hebrew. I worship the Lord, the God of heaven, who has made the sea and the dry land.' Now the sailors are even more afraid because Jonah has admitted that he is fleeing from God, and they ask him what they should do to quieten the storm which is raging even more fiercely.

Gallantly, Jonah tells them to throw him overboard, because he is the cause of the tempest. The sailors must like him well, because they refuse to do this and try their hardest to reach land

and safety. But it is to no avail, and so reluctantly they throw Jonah into the sea. At once the sea grows calm.

God provides a whale to swallow Jonah, and he stays alive in its belly for three days and three nights. Jonah prays to God with great devotion and the whale spews him out onto dry land.

God tells him to go to Nineveh. He walks into the city and cries out, 'Forty days more, and Nineveh shall be destroyed!'

The people of Nineveh believe him. They proclaim a fast, and everyone puts on sackcloth. The king himself rises from his throne, covers himself with sackcloth and ashes, ordering the people to call on God and turn away from violence and wickedness. When God sees what they have done, he relents, and refrains from punishing them.

But Jonah is cross with God. He says, 'O Lord, this is why I fled to Tarshish, for I knew you are a gracious God and merciful, slow to anger, and abounding in steadfast love and ready to relent from punishing. So now I ask to die, for I would rather be dead than alive.' God says to him, 'Is it right for you to be angry?'

Then Jonah goes out of the city and sits down, waiting to see what will happen. God makes a tree grow to shade Jonah from the heat, so now Jonah is very happy. But early next day God causes a worm to attack the bush, so that it withers, and when the sun rises he prepares a sultry east wind. The sun beats down on the head of Jonah so that he feels faint and again begs God to let him die.

God says to Jonah, 'Is it right for you to be angry about the tree?' and Jonah answers, 'Yes, angry enough to die.'

Then the Lord says, 'You are concerned about the tree, for which you did not labour and which you did not grow; it came into being in a night and perished in a night. And should I not be concerned about Nineveh, that great city in which there are more than a hundred and twenty thousand people?'

This is a great story, containing humour and fantasy and a good moral lesson. Jonah is the hero of this comic adventure. God teases him, but in the end teaches him that compassion for people is paramount.

Jonah seems so very different from the other prophets. He is courageous in defying God and tying to run away from him. He is brave and self-sacrificing when he agrees to be thrown overboard to save his companions. He is dogmatic in his opinions and lacking compassion when he disapproves of God's forgiveness of the people of Nineveh, and petulant and sulky when he has to endure the sultry heat in the desert. He is also extraordinarily impudent in his attitude to God, but we hope he finally listened when God explained the importance of forgiveness and compassion.

Is there anything for us to learn from Jonah? His story has the same message as so many of the readings in Lent: that our God is a God of compassion, 'slow to anger and rich in mercy'. But it may be that the story also frees us from being too much afraid of God. We can talk to him like a friend; we can be angry with him and tell him exactly how we feel. Scripture does not say this in so many words, but we can't help thinking that God laughed at the antics of the recalcitrant Jonah.

For personal thought or group discussion:
Do you feel that you have learnt anything from Jonah's story?

Thursday in the First Week of Lent
Esther 4:17; Matthew 7:7-12

In today's reading from Matthew's gospel, Jesus, who is the Way, the Life and the Truth, makes statements which on the face of it are simply not true!

> Ask and you will be given, search and you will find; knock and the door will be opened for you.

Matthew 7:7

The natural human response to this is to say, 'I don't believe it', because experience has shown us that so often when we have pleaded to God for something, our request has been denied.

What, then, are we to make of it? I believe that Jesus is thinking here not of our ordinary lives, where we might ask for money, search for gold, or aim for promotion, but of our spiritual development, of things we might long for in order to become the kind of people God wants us to be.

I am not going to write much today, because I think you may like to use part of your time to reflect on the things you would like to ask for from God to enhance your spiritual life. I have done this exercise for myself:

Dear Lord, I ask you for courage, especially the courage to stand up for what is right. I ask that I may learn to mind less about other people's opinion of me.

Dear Jesus, I am searching for peace of mind and heart. I long to be an instrument of reconciliation for others, but I know that peace has to begin with me.

Dear Loving Father, I knock on the door of opportunity. I ask you to help me to have an open mind and heart and a willingness to embrace new challenges.

As I wrote down these prayers, many other things that I would like to ask for came rushing into my mind, but I guess this is more than enough to ask for just now. Thinking about this has increased my self-awareness, as I hope it will yours.

Friday in the First Week of Lent
Ezekiel 18:21-28; Matthew 5:20-26

Unless your righteousness exceeds that of the scribes and
Pharisees,
you will never enter the kingdom of heaven.
Matthew 5:20

This is what Jesus says at the beginning of today's gospel reading. He is speaking to his disciples. What does he mean by this
and how does it affect us today?

For the Pharisees generally, because not all of them were the
same in their attitudes, what mattered was the upholding of the
law or, as we might put it, keeping the rules. They were out-
raged (or pretended to be) when Jesus broke the law by healing
a man on the Sabbath.

We can see clearly that their attitude was wrong, not to say
ridiculous, but we sometimes don't realise that we too can fall
into the trap of being so diligent about doing everything 'prop-
erly' that we even forget what we are doing it for.

I have vivid memories of a little boy who was about to make
his First Holy Communion. The young catechist felt she had in-
stilled in the child a sense of wonder and a deep love for Jesus,
when an older teacher came along and insisted that the boy
practise walking into church (No slouching! No hands in pock-
ets!). No sooner had he entered the church than there was shout
of rage. The woman stood over the child, glaring down at him.
'How dare you!' she said, 'You think you are fit to receive Our
Lord in Holy Communion and you put your *left* hand in the holy
water stoupe!'

A different translation of Christ's words reads: 'Unless your
virtue goes deeper than that of the scribes and Pharisees.'
Keeping the rules is fine, but only if we realise that when the
rules conflict with compassion, sensitivity, and justice, compassion, sensitivity and justice must always win.

This is an area where, thank God, our churches are getting better. Because we are no longer so rigid in our structures, we are able to move more freely towards uniting with other traditions and understanding other faiths. We can also look beyond our parochial concerns to the needs of the world and the demands of justice.

For personal thought or group discussion:
How important are rules and regulations to you?

Saturday in the First Week of Lent
Deuteronomy 26:16-19; Matthew 5:43-48

Jesus is really challenging us in today's gospel. He is asking us to love our enemies, asking us to be like God our Father, who loves everyone, bad as well as good, unjust as well as just.

We find this hard, or perhaps I should say, I do. I don't have an enemy and I don't hate anyone, but I struggle day in day out to like and to forgive a particularly annoying person who features quite largely in my life. It seems that just when I have brought myself to the brink of loving or forgiving him, he yet again does something that makes me very angry.

I'm sure that many people feel as I do, and struggle to change their feelings. I also realise that my 'enemy' may well be struggling to like and forgive me.

I think one of the reasons we hold on to grudges is that we find it almost impossible to get under the skin of another person, to understand where they are coming from.

Vera was helping with the coffee after Mass, and talking to a parishioner, Celia, a pillar of the church. A young Polish girl, new to the parish, who works in one of the care homes came up to them. 'Please can I have some more biscuits?' Vera gave her two, and was startled to see the quite vicious look on Celia's face. 'The greedy little pig!' she said, 'That's the third lot of biscuits she's had!' Vera shrugged. 'Maybe she's hungry,' she said, 'maybe biscuits are a luxury where she comes from.' But Celia only glowered.

I am still far from succeeding in loving my enemy, but I have discovered that for me the best way to make at least some progress is to pray for him. One of the great things about prayer is that it puts things in perspective. It makes me see how puny and trivial my difficulty is. It reminds me that God really does love my enemy as much as he loves me, and that unlike me he understands why he behaves as he does.

Second Sunday of Lent
Genesis 15:5-12, 17-18; Philippians 3:17-4: 1; Luke 9:28-36

In today's gospel we listened to the story of the Transfiguration. It was a unique event, mysterious and secret. The gospels are full of wonderful happenings, miracles and healings, but the transfiguration of Jesus was different; for those who were present an 'out of this world' experience they would never forget.

In many ways the Transfiguration remains a mystery; there is so little we understand about it. Did Jesus know what was going to happen? Why were only Peter, James and John chosen for this revelation? What was its significance, then and now? There is no way of knowing the answers to such questions.

Peter, James and John had been the daily companions of Jesus for nearly three years. They had perhaps grown used to the revolutionary ideas of his teaching and to the wonders he worked for those who needed healing. They cannot have doubted that he was quite extraordinary, but at the same time he was the familiar friend and brother who shared their hunger, their cold, their sore feet, who walked hundreds of miles as their companion. Perhaps they needed to be shown that he was not just 'someone special', but was the Son of God, fully divine as he was fully human.

For us who love God, there is a tension that mirrors this ambivalence in perception. Our God is remote, immortal, invisible, creator of all that is, to be adored. He is also nearer to us than our breath, he makes his home in us, he identifies with us in our weakness and suffering. It isn't always easy for us to get the balance right, in our praying and our thinking. Perhaps the transfiguration helped Peter, James and John to adjust the balance in their attitude towards Jesus.

Few people have known a transfiguration experience which utterly transformed them. Falling in love may be the nearest most of us get to approaching ecstasy. In nature, too, we sometimes have a glimpse of overwhelming beauty which momentarily stuns us: I think of waking up to discover my whole familiar landscape transformed by a covering of snow, or standing in the cold grey half-light of early morning watching the sun rise from the sea and flood the whole sky with glorious colour. The Transfiguration of Jesus on top of the mountain must have overwhelmed the three disciples with its glory and beauty.

James at the Transfiguration

I didn't want to go with him.
John and Peter were both eager, as always,
but I don't like steep climbs
and I also felt sorry for Andrew.
He is Peter's brother, like I am John's.
Why does Jesus never choose him
to go with him on one of these special expeditions?

But I did go.
It was the way he looked at me.
It's uncanny – he always seems to know
just what you are thinking and feeling.
I thought to myself,
After all, he's just a guy like us, really.
You know someone pretty well
when you've traipsed round Israel with him
for nigh on three years.
I know he's got a way with words –
Some of his stories really get to me –
and he's a great teacher,
but he's only human after all –
I should know –
I've seen him shivering with cold,
aching with hunger,
unsteady for lack of sleep.
And yet – there's something –
something different about him
that makes it impossible to say No.

So we set off.
It was a high mountain, and very steep.
I was slow and found it hard to breathe.
The others kept having to wait for me
and Peter got impatient.

When we reached the summit at last
I threw myself on the ground, panting.
Then I heard a sound
(afterwards I realised it was John, gasping).
I looked up and I saw
Jesus, my Lord, shining in glory.
There were two others with him,
clothed in the same bright raiment.
I knelt before them,
worshipping and adoring.
I was overwhelmed,
fearful and trembling,
but I knew in that moment,
even before the great voice spoke through the cloud,
that Jesus, my friend and companion,
was truly the Son of God.

The church considers the Transfiguration of Our Lord to be such an important feast that this gospel is read twice in the year, once in Lent and again on 6 August. By a strange ironic coincidence, 6 August is also the day when we remember the dropping of the first atomic bomb on Hiroshima. It's impossible to imagine a greater contrast than that between these two events.

On Hiroshima Day we remember the time when man was most degraded, when he sank to the lowest form of cruelty and evil and created a blaze of destruction for thousands of his fellow human beings. Then man came near to hell.

On that day the church celebrates the Feast of the Transfiguration, when Jesus was revealed in glory and on that mountain top the disciples glimpsed for a moment the beauty of God's kingdom. Then man, Peter, James and John, came near to heaven.

We, all of us, contain within us the potential for evil and for good. We can choose hatred and violence or love and peace. By our apathy and indifference, or our vindictiveness, we can drag mankind into an abyss of destruction, or by our concern for our sisters and brothers and our willingness to be involved, we can be candles that burn steadily in the darkness surrounding us, instruments of justice and peace.

For personal thought or group discussion:
Do you think violence can ever be justified?

Monday in the Second Week of Lent
Daniel 9:4-10; Luke 6:36-38

Towards the end of last week, some of the readings were quite tough, hard to live up to. By comparison, Luke's short gospel today seems quite comforting. We are asked to be compassionate, non-judgemental and generous – 'Yes, yes, yes,' may be our immediate response, 'I'll do that gladly, and I'll be rewarded!'

As so often, after a little reflection, we find it is not quite as we thought. Jesus is not asking something easy of us, something that we can achieve without struggle. He is asking us to be like him: not rather compassionate or fairly non-judgemental, but whole-heartedly committed to being his true disciples. It is not, after all, something to be taken lightly.

It's a mistake to think we can strike out on our own and somehow grow into Christ-like people by our own efforts. We need to be bold and brave, full of enthusiasm, ready to embrace newness of life, but I believe we need the Holy Spirit to enlighten, guide, strengthen, console and inspire us, to fill us with his love. We need to set aside time each day to pray, in whatever way suits us best. From the well-spring of this time of prayer we draw the resources we need to work towards becoming compassionate, non-judgemental and generous.

Reflecting on this, I thought about my friends. I am privileged to have many, and they are wonderfully diverse. I asked myself whether any of them came near to being 'of the same mind as Christ Jesus' and in my judgement there are only three, none of them perfect, all of them near to being holy. One is a nun, one a monk and one a married man. Each of them would astonished to be singled out in this way, and would deny that they were holy. They are very different from one another, but each of them is a person committed to a deep prayer life.

For personal thought or group discussion:
Do you know anyone you consider to be truly holy?

Tuesday in the Second Week of Lent
Isaiah 1:10, 16-20; Matthew 23:1-12

'Come now, let us talk this over,'
says the Lord:
'though your sins are like scarlet,
they shall be like snow;
though they are red like crimson,
they shall become like wool.'
Isaiah 1:18

I find it rather comforting, after thinking so much yesterday about holy people, to turn to sinners today! And especially consoling is this image from Isaiah, of 'talking over' things with his people. To me this suggests a couple of friends who can be completely honest with each other, the one listening to the other's concerns. Sometimes, in the Sacrament of Reconciliation, a really good confessor can be like this, listening attentively, trying to understand, not making judgements but making allowances.

The peace which this kind of reconciliation brings can also come about after a walk together in quiet surroundings, an experience which touched me deeply when I worked with young people. It is a wonderful privilege to share our deepest thoughts with a willing friend.

It continues to amaze me that God forgets and forgives our sins so completely, and I find the image of scarlet sins becoming white as snow, crimson sins white as the wool on a lamb's fleece wonderfully reassuring. The feeling of deep peace that is ours when we are reconciled with God, floods us with thankfulness, well-being and renewed energy.

Today's gospel is about humility. Jesus was concerned about the behaviour of the scribes and Pharisees, who failed to live up to their own teaching, and loved to parade in their splendid clothes and take the best seats everywhere and enjoyed being addressed as Rabbi.

It saddens us that our Christian church, which began so simply and humbly, developed into this huge unwieldy institution with an often oppressive hierarchy. Priests, bishops, and cardinals, representatives of Christ, the servant of the people, dress in gorgeous robes and sometimes live in palaces, even though the humblest of their people, at the very bottom of the hierarchy are starving and cruelly oppressed.

It is easy to criticise them, but we have no right to do so until we ourselves are prepared to live among the humblest and fight for their rights.

For personal thought or group discussion:
Do you feel completely forgiven?
Why do you think some churches think it is necessary for their priests to be richly dressed?

Wednesday in the Second Week of Lent
Jeremiah 18:18-20; Matthew 20:17-28

Today's gospel is one of my favourite readings. It's the story of a far-from-impartial mother, which is probably what most mothers are. I remember with some shame how at school Sports Days I would stand on the sidelines and shout myself hoarse, urging my sons to win. And I recall how disappointed I was when my daughter at primary school was not chosen to crown the statue of Mary, even though I myself had suggested another little girl whose mother had recently died! We mothers seem to lose our common sense when it comes to our precious offspring.

So I understand the wife of Zebedee. Even though her sons were grown up and had left home, she still wanted them to be the 'favourites', the most privileged of the disciples and was willing to make something of a fool of herself for their sake.

Of course Jesus was right to be firm with her, as he was with the other disciples who were annoyed with James and John. Whoever wishes to be the first among you must be your slave, he said.

In all walks of life it seems that very few people can hold positions of power without it going to their heads. We see it so often in politics, and even in the church. This makes it all the more impressive to meet someone who could easily rise to a position of authority but chooses instead to take an insignificant role. I think of some of the men in religious orders that I have met who, although they have taken the same vows of chastity, poverty and obedience, decide not to become priests but to serve humbly as brothers. And I have known women of keen intelligence and potential as leaders, who have chosen instead to live 'unseen' in the poorest parts of our cities, working at the most menial jobs, but radiating the love of Christ wherever they go.

For personal thought or group discussion:
Is worldly success important to you?

Thursday in the Second Week of Lent
Jeremiah 17:5-10; Luke 16:19-31

Today we listen to another of Christ's remarkable stories: the one about Dives and Lazarus. I cannot hear it without feelings of guilt and shame and indeed some pity for Dives, the rich man.

I think I feel guilty because I know only too well that I live like Dives, not that I am rich, but because I know that at this moment many people who are my sisters and brothers are dying of starvation, while I, though not feasting on banquets very often, have more than enough to eat, and enjoy a pleasant comfortable lifestyle.

I am writing about myself here, but of course I am only one of millions of people in this western sophisticated world which calls itself the First World, who continue to perpetuate the huge gap which separates the very rich from the very poor.

Feeling guilty is of no use to anyone; there must be something we can do. The campaign for Making Poverty History is a step in the right direction, and very slowly awareness is growing among politicians and people at the grass roots. The people who really make a difference are sadly very few; among them are my friends Paul and Vicky who are going to live in one of the more dangerous countries in Africa, to live and work among the poor. They do not call themselves Christians, but they live like true disciples of Jesus Christ.

As well as this tremendous gap between rich and poor in the world, there is a similar one in our western cities. It is not unusual for people with money, two or three expensive cars, fashionable clothes and elegant houses to live only a hundred metres away from families huddled into dingy bedsits with scarcely any facilities, or indeed from young lost souls sleeping in doorways.

The worst thing about such situations is that the rich people don't even know about the plight of their neighbours, and if it is brought to their notice they are quick to shut their eyes and block their ears. Nobody, and I include myself in this, wants to have to think too much about inequality and poverty. This is one reason why the story Jesus told so powerful: he makes us see the detail in the picture.

There was a rich man who was dressed in purple and fine linen and who feasted sumptuously every day. And at his gate lay a poor man named Lazarus, covered with sores, who longed to satisfy his hunger with what fell from the rich man's table; even the dogs would come and lick his sores.

It would be good if this Lent we could make a special effort to do something towards changing the terrible inequality which we are subscribing to by the way we continue to live. Perhaps it's not enough to put a few extra coins in the box for famine relief. It has been said that charity is the opium of the rich. Maybe we can stay awake, undrugged, unaddicted, so that we can see clearly the path we should take for the sake of our brothers and sisters.

For personal thought or group discussion:
What can *you* do?

Friday in the Second Week of Lent
Genesis 37:3-4, 12-13, 17-28; Matthew 21:33-43, 45-46

It isn't surprising that someone wrote a successful musical called 'Joseph and his Amazing Technicolour Dreamcoat' because the story of Joseph and his brothers makes an exciting drama.

The brothers were for murdering Joseph, because they were jealous of him, but one of them, Reuben, hearing their plot, 'delivered him out of their hands, saying, "Let us not take his life".' Reuben said to them, "Shed no blood, throw him into this pit here in the wilderness, but lay no hand on him" – that he might rescue him out of their hand and restore them to his father.'

I am reminded of the gang warfare that takes place on some estates in our cities. Sometimes one young man shows enough courage to restrain the other gang members from violent action. Such courage is admirable and rare. It is only exceptionally brave people who dare to go against the crowd, especially a gang of boys high on drink or drugs or both.

In the gospel today Jesus is telling a parable which refers to himself. It is a poignant story because of what was going to happen, as Jesus himself was only too aware. When we reflect on the passion of Jesus, particularly in Holy Week, his suffering becomes vividly real to us, but we sometimes forget that he must have been dreading his fate for sometime.

When we need to see a consultant, or go to a hospital for an operation, we often say, 'The waiting is the worst.' Jesus waited alone, and silently, because the disciples simply could not understand what was going to happen. It is already time to mourn for him.

For personal thought or group discussion:
Could you have the courage to stand up and be counted?

Saturday in the Second Week of Lent
Micah 7:14-15, 18-20; Luke 15:1-3, 11-32

We are approaching the halfway mark in this journey of Lent, so perhaps it is a good time to take stock, to look back and see what we have learnt about Jesus and about ourselves. Here are a few questions we could ask ourselves:

Have you learned anything about Jesus that you didn't know before?

Have you learned anything about yourself?

Are there any ways in which you might change?

Are there any actions you would like to take?

Here is a simple Way of the Cross you may like to use for meditation.

The First Station: Jesus is condemned to death.

He is afraid. He is innocent.

What is it like for him to hear the crowds shouting 'Crucify him!'?

The Second Station: Jesus takes up his cross.

He is afraid and vulnerable.

His cross is heavy.

The Third Station: Jesus falls the first time.

He hurts. He is ashamed.

He is angry.

The Fourth Station: Jesus meets his mother.

Jesus finds a moment's consolation.

Jesus feels for his mother.

The Fifth Station: Simon of Cyrene helps Jesus to carry his cross.

Jesus is grateful to Simon.

He blesses Simon. He is afraid he may fall again.

The Sixth Station: Veronica wipes the face of Jesus.

Jesus feels Veronica's compassion.

For a moment he is comforted. He tries to smile but he can't.

The Seventh Station: Jesus falls a second time.
>   Jesus feels weak. He falls and is angry with himself.
>   He is near to despair.

The Eighth Station: Some women of Jerusalem weep for Jesus.
>   Jesus recognises the women. He pities them.
>   He is glad to be upright again.

The Ninth Station: Jesus falls a third time.
>   He feels resigned. He wants to lie on the ground for ever.
>   All his strength has gone.

The Tenth Station: Jesus is stripped of his clothes.
>   Jesus feels humiliated.
>   He thinks of others who have suffered humiliation.

The Eleventh Station: Jesus is nailed to the cross.
>   The pain is terrible.
>   He cries out. He is very afraid.

The Twelfth Station: Jesus dies on the cross.
>   Jesus is thirsty.
>   He looks on his mother with love.
>   He responds to the repentant thief.
>   He cries out, near to despair.
>   He forgives his tormentors.
>   He gives himself up to his Father.

The Thirteenth Station: Jesus' body is taken down from the cross.
>   Mary cradles Jesus.
>   His friends bathe and anoint him.

The Fourteenth Station: Jesus is buried.
>   It is dark.
>   It is silent.
>   The tomb is closed.
>   He is dead.

At each station, you may like to change some of the words and/or add some of your own. You could also write a prayer to go with each station.

Third Sunday of Lent
Exodus 3:1-8, 13-15; Corinthians 10:1-6, 10-12; Luke 13: 1-9

I went to see my friend Anna in her new house, and I was surprised when, just as I was about to step into the hall from the porch, she said, 'Would you mind taking off your shoes?'

Of course I didn't mind at all, but as I stepped in stocking feet onto the beautifully polished oak floor, I remember silently asking myself, Is this holy ground, then?

The encounter of Moses with God in the burning bush which we hear at Mass today, is very moving: the complete surrender in humility of Moses before the Lord. And I am moved myself when I enter a sacred building, church, chapel, temple, synagogue or mosque and become instantly aware of my own littleness before the presence of God. I am very happy then to take off my shoes.

But to return to Anna, her new house was delightful and it was good to see her pleasure in it. I understood her desire to keep it as perfect as possible, to preserve her beautiful flooring and carpets from the scruffs and stains of outdoor footwear.

After we had inspected the house we sat in the living room and over tea and cake talked as old friends do about everything and nothing. I began to feel completely at home and relaxed as I always do with Anna, and very soon the anxieties and uncertainties about a crisis in my life began tumbling out in an unstoppable stream. Anna listened patiently and quietly and when at last I got up to go she held me close for a few moments in a warm embrace.

Later that night, I was mulling over my visit to Anna, when a thought struck me. I had nearly laughed at Anna, because she asked me to remove my shoes, but now I realised that in her house I was walking on holy ground, because I was in the presence of someone in whom the God of compassion makes its home.

I firmly believe that our God is not only to be found in places that are officially holy. He (or she) is present wherever there is love and loving-kindness. We human beings do well when we learn not just to respect but to reverence one another, for we never know when we are walking on holy ground.

Today's psalm is one of the most beautiful and one of those particularly appropriate for Lent. Only part of the psalm is read at Mass, so I will write it out a little more fully here so that we can reflect on it again. It is a hymn of praise to our God who is so ready to forgive and abounding in love and compassion.

Bless the Lord, O my soul,
and all that is within me,
bless his holy name.
Bless the Lord, O my soul,
and do not forget all his blessings,
who forgives all your iniquity,
who heals all your diseases,
who redeems your life from the Pit,
who crowns you with steadfast love and mercy,
who satisfies you with good as long as you live
so that your youth is renewed
like the eagle's.

The Lord is merciful and gracious,
slow to anger and abounding in steadfast love ...
He does not deal with us according to our sins,
nor repay us according to our iniquities.
For as the heavens are high above the earth,
So great is his steadfast love towards those who fear him;
as far as the east is from the west,
so far he removes our transgressions from us.
as a father has compassion for his children,
so the Lord has compassion for those who fear him.
Psalm 102 (103):1-5, 8-13

The gospel today contains the short parable of the fig tree. This emphasises the value Jesus places on fruitfulness. Perhaps second only to his command that we should love one another is his desire that we should use our gifts to bear fruit.

Some people might say: How can I be fruitful? Look at me! I am too old, I am disabled, I have learning difficulties, I am weighed down with problems. But being fruitful does not necessarily mean achieving things. It is wiser perhaps to look at the fruits of the Holy Spirit for guidance. '... The fruit of the Spirit is love, joy, peace, patience, kindness, generosity, faithfulness, gentleness and self-control' (Galatians 5:22). Perhaps that's enough to be working on!

For personal thought or group discussion:
Is there any place where you felt you were walking on holy ground?
Jesus wanted us to be fruitful. In what ways do you succeed in this?

Monday in the Third Week of Lent
Exodus 17:1-7; John 4:5-42

There is so much in today's gospel reading that we could study it for weeks. There is also much that is odd about it. Although the encounter of Jesus with the Samaritan woman is full of meaning and has more than one compelling message, John is the only gospel writer to describe it. It was unusual for Jesus to talk to a woman on his own, and his disciples were surprised at this, but what made it really puzzling was that it was a Samaritan woman. Jews and Samaritans generally hated each other. Bad enough to speak to a woman on your own, but a Samaritan woman? That was beyond a joke. However, as we know, Jesus was no conformist, and we know from other gospel accounts that he enjoyed the company of women.

It is interesting to compare the account of this meeting with two other powerful gospel narratives which we have already read this Lent. The Prodigal Son gospel is a story, not a factual account, although we are so carried along by the momentum of the story that it's easy to forget that it wasn't an actual happening. One of the most striking themes of both the Prodigal Son and the Samaritan woman is forgiveness (which is of course a central theme in the whole of Lent) but from very different aspects.

The story Jesus told is charged with emotion; the father and son hug and kiss in a moment of fervent reconciliation; interestingly no woman is mentioned. On the other hand, a woman is the focus of Jesus when he meets her by the well in Samaria; there is no overt emotion; the exchange is cool and disciplined though the repercussions of her being forgiven are more far-reaching.

It is also worthwhile to turn our attention to the Transfiguration; the disciples see Jesus utterly changed, transfigured in light, glorious. In Samaria with Jesus, the woman is changed utterly. There is nothing physical to see, but she has become another

56

person, her life is turned upside down, she experiences a true conversion, she is repentance personified, and most importantly, a real evangeliser, drawing others to Jesus.

The well is central to the story of Jesus and the Samaritan woman. It was the source of living water, but Jesus, who was to cry out from his agony on the cross 'I thirst!', was and is the source of water that gives new life to the soul. He is a spring of living water, and he said, 'Let anyone who is thirsty come to me, and let the one who believes in me drink' (John 7: 37). The Samaritan woman did believe him.

A 'Good' Woman of Sychar

I used not to know her name,
but I'd heard of her, of course.
Notorious was the word for her.
I'd seen her once or twice too,
and I have to admit
she must have been a beauty once.
But all those men!
She was shameless.

Which made it all the more surprising
when she came running into town that day,
all flushed and excited and begging us
to go and see this man she'd met.
Another man! I sighed, and groaned,
But I was curious.

Some of us went with her,
and we saw him,
the strange Jew.
We listened to him,
and the rest is history.

I used not to know her name,
but I do now.
It was through her I met
the Saviour of the world.

Tuesday in the Third Week of Lent
Daniel 3:25, 34-43; Matthew 18:21-35

The concept of forgiveness features very largely in the gospels and in Lent. First, we are assured of God's forgiveness, our scarlet sins becoming whiter than snow, then we ourselves are exhorted to forgive, over and over again, not just forty-nine times, but for as long as it takes.

Then, in today's gospel, we are told, by means of one of Christ's dramatic stories, that we cannot expect forgiveness unless we ourselves are ready to forgive. 'Forgive us our trespasses, as we forgive those who trespass against us.' We recite these words, perhaps more than once each day, but do we really think of what we are saying? If we do, we will know it isn't easy. Some people hurt us deeply, say they are sorry then do it all over again. Our reserves of patience, sympathy and understanding are exhausted.

Therein lies the difference between God and us. No matter how often we break our promises and repeat the same wrongs, his reserves of patience, sympathy and understanding never run dry.

Some people find it extremely hard to forgive. And who would blame the victims of torture, the mothers of children who have been brutally raped and/or murdered, those who have been cruelly rejected or ruthlessly betrayed? Perhaps only those who have endured similar suffering have the right to criticise the unforgiving.

Anthony Walker, a bright, intelligent, loving and lovable teenager, was viciously murdered by a blow from an axe, just because he was black. The people of Britain were stunned and horrified. But they were arguably far more stunned when a few days later his mother publicly declared that she forgave Anthony's murderers. To the astonished bystanders, she explained, struggling with her emotions, that she forgave them because that's what Jesus did when he was dying on the cross. There is no question that Mrs Walker greatly loved her son, but in that moment, her courage and generosity of spirit drew her to be 'of the same mind as Christ Jesus'.

For personal thought or group discussion:
What is your reaction to Mrs Walker's declaration of forgiveness?

Wednesday in the Third Week of Lent
Deuteronomy 4:1, 5-9; Matthew 5:17-19

Both the first reading and the gospel today are about the importance of keeping the law. Moses is speaking to the people just before they enter the promised land, and in the gospel Jesus is talking to his disciples, telling them not to imagine that he has come to do away with the law.

Whether as citizens or members of a church, we need the structure of the law because without it there would be chaos. However, this does not mean that the law should be entirely rigid, never making allowances for particular circumstances. A starving child is certainly entitled to break the law by stealing bread or money. Jesus himself seems to have broken the law quite often when someone's need or suffering required it. Even though it was the Sabbath, he did not hesitate to cure the man with a withered hand.

Sometimes the law can be a minefield, and it is difficult to see our way clear. What to us seems manifestly right, may be illegal. The laws of the church are intended to guide us safely towards the kingdom of heaven, but it can happen that we become so obsessed with obeying the letter of the law that we lose sight of the greatest law of all, the law of love which supercedes every other.

One of the Pharisees asked Jesus a question:
'Teacher, which commandment in the law is the greatest?' Jesus said to him, 'You shall love the Lord your God with all your heart, and with all your soul, and with all your mind. This is the greatest and first commandment. And the second is like it: You shall love your neighbour as yourself. On these two commandments hang all the law and the prophets.' (Matthew 22:36-40)

A refugee family had lived in the parish for three years. They settled happily and took a full part in parish activities. The children, in spite of language difficulties, were doing well at school.

Then one morning, with no warning, a letter arrived from the Home Office saying they were to be deported to their country of origin. This was a terrible shock. The father, Michael, had been tortured and threatened with death in Sri Lanka; his wife, Cynthia, had been raped repeatedly. They were terrified and bewildered. They had been so certain they would be given permission to stay. Michael phoned Maggie, a volunteer at the local drop-in centre for refugees and asylum seekers, and she came round at once.

She tried to reassure the family, saying, 'Don't worry, we'll do all we can to help you. Pack everything you need and stay here until after dark. Someone will come for you then.'

At eight o'clock Maggie and her husband, Jim, arrived with a van. They drove the family round to the Catholic church where the young priest, Father Eddie, met them. A big tall man, he held out his arms and enveloped the whole family in a warm hug. Then he took them into the sacristy of his church. To their surprise, another family was there, a mother and her teenage sons from Zimbabwe. There were mattresses on the floor and a plate of sandwiches on the table.

'You'll be safe here,' Father Eddie said.

The children slept, but Michael and Cynthia lay awake. Early next morning they heard banging and shouting, then Father Eddie's voice, firm and clear.

'This is the house of God. You enter it over my dead body!'

The immigration officer shouted back angrily: 'You realise you're breaking the law, Father?'

'Yes,' answered the priest. 'And do you realise you're breaking the law of love?'

The families are still there. But for how long?

For personal thought or group discussion:
Do you think Father Eddie was right?

Thursday in the Third Week of Lent
Jeremiah 7:23-28; Luke 11:14-23

In today's first reading, God is lamenting the fact that the people will not listen to his voice. In Mark's gospel, Jesus says, 'Do you have ears, and fail to hear?' (Mark 8:18).

We, too, are not very dependable when it comes to listening to God's word. Reading scripture, or listening to it in church, or perhaps listening to an excellent preacher or retreat giver, we often don't give our full attention to what is being said. We are distracted, both by serious worries and trivial thoughts; our concentration is poor. Yet absorbing the word of God, or the words of an inspiring speaker, is so important for our growth as Christians.

The same thing applies to prayer, our other source of spiritual nourishment. If we don't open our hearts and minds to God in our attitude of listening when we give the time for prayer, we risk becoming static and stunted, unfulfilled and unfruitful, not what God wants for his people.

Listening is altogether an undervalued skill. As well as listening to God, we need to listen to one another, really listen.

Ursula, a friend of Penny's, telephoned her, sounding very distressed. She asked Penny to go round to see her.

'I've got to talk to someone,' she said, 'I'm desperate for some advice.' Penny didn't want to go. She didn't think she had the right skills. She certainly wouldn't feel happy to give advice – about anything. But Ursula really did sound desperate, and she hadn't the heart to turn her down.

Penny was shocked when she saw Ursula's face. It was dreadful to see her looking so wretched. She offered Penny coffee or tea, but she said No, and almost at once they sat down and Ursula began to talk.

She talked and she cried, talked and wept, talked and sobbed. Penny said nothing. She felt completely inadequate. She could not imagine there was anything she could do to help Ursula. She felt worse than useless, and wished she hadn't agreed to come.

At length Ursula stopped talking and dried her eyes. She even managed a small smile. Then to Penny's surprise, she said, 'I can never thank you enough. You've been absolutely, marvellous. I feel so much better, thanks to you. I'll never forget this, Penny.' Completely baffled, Penny got away as soon as she could.

A few days later, without mentioning Ursula's name, Penny described what had happened to another friend who happened to be a counsellor. 'The oddest thing is that I never said a single word!' Penny finished.

Her friend smiled. 'You must be a very good listener.' she said.

What happened to Penny is not so unusual. Even when people are extremely upset, they sometimes find that just being with someone unthreatening who gives them their full attention, goes a long way towards healing their distress.

For personal thought or group discussion:
Are you a good listener – to God and to others?

Friday in the Third Week of Lent
Hosea 14:2-10; Mark 12:28-34

The Scribe who questioned Jesus

I knew that the others, well some of them, and particularly the Pharisees, wouldn't like it. They would see it as letting the side down, or fraternising with the enemy.

But it wasn't like that. I just found him so fascinating to listen to. He drew me like a magnet. He wasn't a polished speaker, like so many of our people, but you could sense his complete integrity, the truth of him.

So when I spoke up, I was not so much afraid of what the scribes and Pharisees would think as I was of his reaction to me. But I needn't have worried; he was fine. He answered me courteously and fully, and I told him what I thought. Then he said something I will never forget:

'Your are not far from the kingdom of God.'

He could not have said anything more pleasing to me than that.

Usually in the gospels we see the scribes and Pharisees as being highly suspicious of Jesus and fiercely hostile to him. However, this scribe is different; he has a fruitful exchange with Jesus and they admire one another. I can't help wondering what this scribe's thoughts were later on when Jesus was crucified.

To be told by Jesus that he was not far from the kingdom of God must have felt like a special blessing to the scribe. But what did Jesus mean by 'the kingdom' and what do we mean by it? Is it a place, another name for heaven, or is a state of being?

Although it isn't easy to define exactly what the kingdom is, the most likely explanation seems to be that it is where the people of God come into their own: a place of blessedness and peace. In today's first reading from Hosea, there is a beautiful picture of what it may be like for Israel, and for us, when 'God's anger towards us is no more.' Perhaps it is a description of how it will be for those who live in the Kingdom?

I will love them freely,
for my anger has turned from them.
I will be like dew to Israel;
he shall blossom like the lily,
he shall strike root like the forests of Lebanon.
His shoots shall spread out;
His beauty shall be like the olive tree,
And his fragrance like that of Lebanon.
They shall again live beneath my shadow,
they shall flourish as a garden;
they shall blossom like the vine,
their fragrance shall be like the wine of Lebanon.

For personal thought or group discussion:
What do *you* imagine the Kingdom is like?

Saturday in the Third Week of Lent
Hosea 5:15-6: 6; Luke 18:9-14

The Pharisee

It was a revelation.
It happened after I had prayed.
I was leaving the temple
and I happened to glance across
at that wretched tax-collector.
It was just the look on his face.
He wasn't wretched after all.
He was truly at peace.
I saw that he was blessed
in a way I had never been.
I knew I had missed something
absolutely vital.
So I went back into the temple.
I said nothing.
I simply stood in the presence of our God
until it slowly dawned on me,
the truth about myself:
my pride, my contempt
my self-righteousness.
I knew then that I was a sinner,
and I asked the Lord for mercy.

I stayed a long time in the temple,
and when I walked away,
I knew there was just a chance
that one day my face too
might be like that tax-collector's,
glowing with peacefulness
and quiet happiness.

In one translation of this parable, we read that Jesus was telling it to 'some people who prided themselves on being virtuous and despised everyone else.'

There are still people like that in our churches today, who think in terms of 'bad people out there'. All of us have to be careful not to imagine that because we are Christians and church-goers, we are somehow better than other people. It is all too obvious that we are not, particularly if, like the Pharisee in the story, we hold others in contempt.

For personal thought or group discussion:
Do you find it hard to confess your sins to God?
Do you feel at peace afterwards?

Fourth Sunday of Lent
Joshua 5:9-12; Corinthians 5:17-21; Luke 15:1-3, 11-32

This day is known as Laetare Sunday, *laetare* meaning 'Rejoice' or 'Be happy'. It is a day for dwelling not so much on our sins and our unworthiness as on the joy of belonging to Christ and the joy of being forgiven.

The psalm is full of confidence:

I sought the Lord and he answered me
and delivered me from all my fears.
Look to him, and be radiant;
So your faces shall never be ashamed.
The poor soul cried, and was heard by the Lord,
and was saved from every trouble.
Psalm 33 (34):4-6

It is also the day when it is usual to celebrate Mother's Day or Mothering Sunday, so the happiness and thankfulness we feel in being forgiven, welcomed and loved by God, can overflow into the happiness we owe to our mothers and the thankfulness we feel towards them. However, we need to be beware of complacency. Not everyone has a happy relationship with their mother, and some women have a passionate longing to *be* mothers. It is not easy for those who are in such situations to feel radiant and joyous when they see small children giving flowers to their mothers. In the bible there are many instances of women who were despised because they were barren and yearned to have a child: Hannah, Sarah and Elizabeth among them. It is an issue that requires sensitivity.

If there were a competition for the 'greatest story ever told', the Prodigal Son would be in with a chance. We may have heard it over and over again, but there is a wealth of inspiration from different aspects of the story. The characters are so real that we sometimes forget that Jesus, describing the father, is describing his Father, the all-compassionate, whose love for repentant sinners is unconditional and whole-hearted.

The father in the story, evidently a wealthy landowner, would have been expected to behave with restraint and dignity. But not this father. He couldn't sit around waiting for his son's return; he kept a constant watch, never losing faith that some day his son would come home.

When at last he saw him in the distance, he ran, met him, clasped him in his arms and ordered an impromptu party with the killing of the fatted calf, music and dancing. At the time when Jesus told this story it was absolutely not done for a respectable man to show his ankles, something that the father could not have avoided as he lifted his robe to run. In other words, nothing at all can prevent the outpouring of God's love on those who ask his forgiveness. We feel humbled and ashamed in the face of such generosity; our hearts are full of gratitude, and we are at peace. How shall we respond?

The Elder Son
It may be the most powerful story ever told,
one of the greatest dramas,
and I had the bit part.
I was not so much the villain
as the one people don't much like,
cursed with so many unattractive attributes:
jealousy, envy, sulkiness
and what to me at least
was the moral high ground.

But I wonder
how many of the countless men and women
who listened to the story
and ended up loving the Prodigal Son
and adoring our Father,
I wonder how many of them are honest enough
to recognise themselves
not in my wayward brother,
but in me.

If I were alive today
in the twenty-first century,
you would respect me,
you would know me for an upright man
driven by the Christian work ethic,
uncompromising, loyal,
law-abiding,
but not so forgivable
as my young brother.

I am sorry,
sorry for being so miserable,
sorry for failing to see
that I don't matter all that much,
that dogma and doctrine don't matter
all that much,
that the life of the Holy Spirit can flourish and grow
when the human spirit expands and responds
and knows how to celebrate reconciliation.

For personal thought or group discussion:
What do you think about the elder son in the story?

Monday in the Fourth Week of Lent
Micah 7:7-9; John 9:1-41

Today's gospel is the account of the man born blind. Whenever I come across the word 'blindness' I think of the blind children I have known. Possibly by some odd coincidence, they were all positive, cheerful and courageous.

I remember a particular incident with Tilly. She was five years old at the time, blind and confined to a wheelchair because of spina bifida. I had undertaken to present a small class of five-year-olds in a morning assembly in front of the whole school. We planned it carefully and practised hard. It was the first time a class so young had led the assembly, and we were anxious for it to go well. The children were all excited as we guided them up the ramp onto the stage. Tilly was placed in the centre, and as her voice was strong and clear she had a major part in the production.

The assembly was a great success and there was enthusiastic applause for the children for doing so well and then I said, 'You can go back to your classroom.'

At once Tilly released her brakes and zoomed straight ahead and off the stage, her wheelchair plunging dangerously to the floor and landing with its back wheels in the air. I had forgotten to tell her to wait for someone to guide her. I rushed over and with others righted her chair. Tilly was flushed and one of her hands was cut. 'Tilly, I'm so sorry. Are you all right?' She smiled. 'Yes, Miss, I'm fine,' she said.

The Man Born Blind
It was the most wonderful thing
that could ever have happened to me.
I opened my eyes and saw
all the things I had only imagined till now.
The light and the colour dazzled me
and I felt overwhelmed, bewildered

71

at the sight of so many people,
so many different people milling around.

For a moment I looked only at him,
Jesus, who was my saviour.
His face was gentle and strong;
I felt that his eyes reached
To the very depths of my soul.
What happened to me was a miracle,
yet it was simple and straightforward.
Jesus touched my eyes and healed me.
Now I could see.

The Pharisees made it all so complicated.
They asked me what happened; I told them.
They asked me what I thought of him; I told them.
Then they dragged my parents in.
They were both frightened,
So they passed the buck to me.
That's why I told them straight.
'If this man were not from God
he could do nothing.'
They drove me away then,
But Jesus found me.
I looked at him again;
I trusted him completely.
I said, 'Lord, I believe'
and I worshipped him.

There is a sense in which most of us are blind, blind to the plight of the needy and deaf to the cry of the poor. We live our lives in a bubble of security and comfort. We can manage our own little world; it is clean and tidy, safe from the intrusion of challenge.

If, through indifference or cowardice, we don't open our eyes and face what is happening outside our narrow comfort zone, we will remain, like the talent the slave buried in the ground, of no use to God or man.

Tuesday in the Fourth Week of Lent
Ezekiel 47:1-9, 12; John 5:1-3, 5-16

Whenever we receive a bottle of pills, there is a piece of paper with instructions enclosed with them. It is the same with any kit we buy, any new car, bicycle or lawn mower. These instructions are often baffling and frustrating, but they are also necessary, if we want to take the medicine in the right quantity and at the right time, if we want our new machine to work.

Sometimes we feel the need of some sort of definite guidance in our spiritual lives, and we might be glad of them if we are seriously taking this journey through Lent. St Paul was certainly convinced of the value of 'instructions', and when he wrote this powerful message to the Colossians he was giving them a guide to the Christian life which is just as valid for us today:

... clothe yourselves with compassion, kindness, gentleness and patience. Bear with one another and if anyone has a complaint against another, forgive each other; just as the Lord has forgiven you, so you also must forgive. Above all, clothe yourselves with love, which binds everything together in perfect harmony. And let the peace of Christ rule your hearts, to which indeed you were called in the body. And be thankful. Let the word of Christ dwell in you richly; teach and advise one another in all wisdom; and with gratitude in your hearts sing psalms, hymns and spiritual songs to God. And whatever you do, in word or deed, do everything in the name of the Lord Jesus, giving thanks to God the Father through him (Colossians 3: 12-17).

It is worth reading this passage slowly and thoughtfully. You may like to choose one or two 'instructions' to reflect and pray about. You may find a particular strength or weakness of yours high-lighted in Paul's letter.

Wednesday in the Fourth Week of Lent
Isaiah 49:8-15; John 5:17-30

A woman I didn't know very well was confiding in me. She was miserable and lonely. Rather boldly I asked her if she believed in God. Her face lit up. 'Oh, yes!' she said, and pointing upwards added, 'I know he's up there, watching me with his big stick!' She was clearly quite fond of God as she imagined him.

I tried, probably in vain, to explain to her that God is very different from her idea of him. I didn't have a bible with me, otherwise I might have read to her from the end of today's reading from Isaiah:

... the Lord has comforted his people,
and will have compassion on his suffering ones.
But Zion said, 'The Lord has forsaken me,
my Lord has forgotten me.'
Can a woman forget her child at her breast,
or show no compassion to the child of her womb?
Even these may forget,
yet I will not forget you.
See, I have inscribed you on the palms of my hands.

This passage always stands out from the text for me because I find it such a tender and convincing portrayal of the God I believe in. I know that there are other places in the Old Testament where the writers see God as not at all like this, but angry, vengeful, even brutal. I could be charged with cherry-picking from scripture only the 'nice bits', the parts which fit in with my own beliefs.

But I have chosen extracts like this one because it shows an understanding of God which comes to fulfillment in the life of Jesus, and in the words of the New Testament.

Jesus said, 'Are not two sparrows sold for a penny?

Yet not one of them will fall to the ground without your Father knowing it.
And even the hairs on your head are all counted.'
(Matthew 10: 29-30)

And in the first letter of John we read:
Beloved, let us love one another, because love is from God; everyone who loves is born of God and knows God. Whoever does not love does not know God, for God is love. God's love was revealed among us in this way: God sent his only Son into the world so that we might live through him. In this is love, not that we loved God but that he loved us and sent his Son to be an atoning sacrifice for our sins.
(1 John 4:7-10; John 5: 31-47)

For personal thought or group discussion:
Some of the Old Testament writers had a very different view of God from the one we have learned to believe in through getting to know Jesus. Is there any passage in scripture which convinces you of God's love for you?

Thursday in the Fourth Week of Lent
Exodus 32:7-14; John 5:31-47

Barney and Dave worked together on a building site. Barney had a wife and two small children, Dave lived alone. At the end of the week, they received the same wages. Just before Christmas, on pay day, Dave suggested they should go to the pub for a drink. Barney's face fell. He looked embarrassed and miserable.

'Sorry, mate', he said, 'some other time, eh?' He turned to go, but Dave caught hold of his sleeve.

'Just the one, Barney,' he said, 'and it's my shout. You must have a hell of a lot of expense at this time of year.'

Minutes later they were sitting in a corner of the bar drinking their beer. Barney began to talk. 'I'm dead worried, Dave,' he said. 'We're in a mess, me and Linda. We're up to our necks in debt. She gets those catalogues and buys all sorts of rubbish we can't afford, and we owe more than a grand.' He put his head in his hands. 'I don't know what to do, Dave. It's going to be a rotten Christmas for the kids. I just can't afford to buy them presents.'

Dave was very sorry. He couldn't think how to help Barney. He bought another couple of drinks and they sat in silence for a while. Then Dave asked, 'How old are the children?' 'Ellie's six and April is four,' Barney answered.

'It's just a thought,' Dave said, 'but you could try the Citizens Advice. I think they can really help with debt problems.'

Barney brightened a little. 'Thanks, Dave,' he said, 'I'll give it a try.'

Dave spent the next ten evenings after work in his cellar, making a doll's house. He always liked making things and he knew where to go for both materials and ideas. He became so absorbed in the project that sometimes he forgot to have any supper.

By Christmas Eve the little house was finished, brightly painted and filled with tiny pieces of furniture. It was also sturdy, not easy to break. Dave looked at it and sighed with satisfaction. Then he placed it carefully in a big cardboard box, covered the box with cheerful wrapping paper and fixed a clearly printed label on it.

On the label he had written, in block capitals:
HAPPY CHRISTMAS
ELLIE AND APRIL
WITH LOVE FROM
FATHER CHRISTMAS

After dark, he took the box round to Barney's house, placed it on the doorstep and rang the bell. Then he slipped away out of sight.

The reason Dave went to so much trouble was that he cared a lot for his friend. After the first few nights he began to enjoy the work, although he hadn't undertaken it for his own pleasure. Nor had he done it in the hope of Barney's gratitude and praise. He wasn't interested in Barney's approval: only in his happiness and that of his children.

In today's gospel, Jesus, speaking to the Jews, says, 'I do not accept glory from human beings.' (In other translations: 'As for human approval, this means nothing to me.') When I read this, I sighed, because I not only like human approval, I positively seek it. I like it when people pay me compliments and say agreeable things about me. If I had spent all the time on a doll's house that Dave did, I would have rung that doorbell and handed over the parcel with a self-deprecating smile, if not a flourish!

My guess is that a lot more people are like me than are like Dave. It is a very human failing, but a failing nonetheless. At the very beginning of Lent, in the gospel on Ash Wednesday, Jesus has some salutary words about this:

Beware of practising your piety before others in order to be seen by them; for then you have no reward from your Father in heaven. So whenever you give alms, do not sound a trumpet before you, as the hypocrites do in the synagogues and in the streets, so that they may be praised by others ... But whenever you give alms, do not let your left hand know what your right hand is doing, so that your alms may be done in secret; and your Father who sees in secret will reward you (Matthew 6: 1-4).

For personal thought or group discussion:
Does human approval mean a lot to you?

Friday in the Fourth Week of Lent
Wisdom 2:1, 12-22; John 7:1-2, 10:25-30

In today's extract from the book of Wisdom, we read the words of the godless:

> Let us test him with insult and torture, so that we may find out how gentle he is and make a trial out of his forbearance. Let us condemn him to a shameful death. (v19, 20)

These words make us think of Jesus and those who pursued him so vindictively, the men whose wickedness blinded them, who did not know the 'hidden things of God'. And when I think of those last days before his inevitable crucifixion, and Jesus hounded by the men with power, then into my mind comes the image of Robert.

Robert is a prisoner on Death Row. We write to each other. I tell him about my life and he gives me glimpses into his, though so little happens to him beyond the dreary round of his solitary days that he finds it difficult to vary his letters. He says he is innocent of the crime for which he is being punished, and he knows his young life is doomed to be cut short.

Like Jesus, Robert faces the near-certainty of death with courage. Like Jesus, he expresses his love for God his father, and his concern for others. Jesus was afraid, and at times, lonely. Robert is afraid, and except for the weekly visit of a prison chaplain, lonely all the time.

Here is an extract from one of his letters:

> 'As I write this letter, I hope and pray that it finds you in the best of health and spirits ... I've got you in my prayer daily ... at times I feel so very low, but I must not give up because of my mother and dad. Whenever I just want to give up I turn to our Lord Jesus Christ ... I do what I can to survive, with Jesus giving me comfort and giving me strength.'

I find it very humbling to read these letters. I do not for a moment suggest that Robert's suffering is anything like as terrible as Christ's was, and I have no way of knowing whether or not he is innocent of the crime for which he must pay. But I am struck by the way his situation resembles that of Jesus, and by the courage and absolute trust in God that is common to them both.

For personal thought or group discussion:
Would you like to visit someone in prison, or write to someone on Death Row?

Saturday in the Fourth Week of Lent
Jeremiah 11:18-20; John 7:40-52

Nicodemus

I know I am a coward
theres's no two ways about it.
Oh – I'm good at making excuses to myself
'If you want to have influence with the others,
you have to play along with them.'
And I do. Anyone will tell you
I'm a decent chap,
not one to rock the boat,
a safe pair of hands
and all the rest of the clichés.
So I'm not only a coward,
but a hypocrite too
pretending to be something other than I am,
a dependable conformist,
not rash enough to question
the conduct of my betters.

Once or twice I've tried,
tried to be true to myself.
I even plucked up the courage
To visit Jesus once.
I went by night
so nobody would see me.
I had secretly admired him
and respected his teaching
for a considerable time. But when I met him
I loved him.

Jesus changed me.
I saw things now through different eyes
and privately longed to be one of his people
instead of one of the powerful.

Yet it was only at the moment
when they wanted to arrest him
that I found my voice,
my dissenting voice, at last.
I, Nicodemus, dared to question
their authority.
They mocked me, then,
And it did me no harm.
It was Jesus who suffered harm.

And now, too late,
I have done what I can.
I, who so weakly failed him in life,
have honoured him in death.

For personal thought or group discussion:
What is your opinion of Nicodemus?

Fifth Sunday of Lent
Isaiah 43:16-21; Philippians 3: 8-14; John 8: 1-11

Last Sunday we listened to the great gospel of forgiveness, the story of the Prodigal Son, and today we have a similar theme in John's account of the woman caught in the act of adultery. In a very few simple words, Jesus demolishes judgementalism and encourages self-awareness. He doesn't pretend that the woman is innocent, for he tells her not to sin any more, but he saves her from the vindictiveness of the self-righteous men. The Pharisees come to the realisation that they are sinners too.

Today, so many centuries later, we are still quick to judge and vilify what we perceive to be sexual sins. In our righteous indignation we can be quite blind to our own sinfulness, to our lack of integrity, generosity and love.

Sadly, it happens that even in our churches we get our priorities wrong. We sincerely want to be good Catholics, or good Protestants and so we strive to keep all the rules, and sometimes become so obsessed with our own spiritual progress that we fail to notice what is going on in the lives of those around us.

Pat's parish priest was a stickler for the rules: he forbade the people to talk to one another before or after Mass, because they might disturb others who were praying. 'If you want to speak to anyone, talk to God,' he said. Pat was a perfectionist; she wanted to obey the priest whom she admired.

And so it happened one Sunday after Mass that when her friend Claudia came to sit next to her, Pat took no notice and continued to pray. After a few moments Caludia tapped her on the shoulder. Pat wasn't pleased. 'Can't you see I'm praying?' she asked, then realising that Claudia was obviously distressed, she whispered, 'Look, give me a call tonight.'

Claudia didn't call. The following day she went to a clinic for an abortion and that evening telephoned Pat. In between sobs she told her what she had done. Pat's first reaction was anger. 'How could you!' she said. 'You know it's a terrible sin. I can't believe you did it. Why didn't you tell me you were thinking of it?' 'I tried to,' Claudia said. 'I was sure you would help me, advise me. But you wouldn't listen. You said you were praying. I was so scared, Pat, I didn't know what to do. I felt so alone. But oh, Pat I do wish I hadn't done it!'

Now Pat was crying too. 'I was just about to go to Mass,' she said, 'but I'll come round to you now instead.'

The Eldest Pharisee
God knows I have tried,
ever since I was a little child,
to do what is right.
As I grew older,
I immersed myself in the law.
I believed what it says in the psalms,
that the law is more to be desired than gold,
and sweeter than honey.
I was uneasy about the man, Jesus,
but I didn't want to trick him.
I was curious to see what he was like,
even to listen to his teaching.
So I went along with the others
When they caught the young woman.
I didn't really look at her,
not at first. I was struck by Jesus,
his stillness, the way he seemed quite unfazed
when we challenged him.
While we waited for his answer,
I glanced at her.
I saw she was absolutely terrified,
and I forgot what a sinner she was –
I even found myself feeling sorry,
for her, an adultress!
So when he spoke at last, so gravely, saying,
'Let anyone among you who is without sin
be the first to throw a stone at her,'
I didn't hesitate. I was the first to walk away.

Monday in the Fifth Week of Lent
2 Kings 4:18-21, 32-37; John 11:1-45

There is so much in the story of Lazarus that we could spend hours, perhaps even a whole day, reflecting on it and wondering about the questions that arise from those reflections.

First, we might wonder why, when Jesus hears that Lazarus, the one his sisters describe as 'the man you love' is ill, he decides to stay where he is for two more days. Then we might consider Martha and Mary. Why did Martha go out to meet Jesus while Mary stayed at home? What was the relationship like between Jesus and that small family? We are told that he loved them all. Clearly it was good for Martha, Mary and Lazarus to have Jesus as their close friend, and it was probably good for him too, to have a warm friendship with people not directly involved in his ministry. Celibate priests seem to be enriched by the loving support of lay people.

Then there is Thomas. He is one of the twelve disciples we know little about, though he is remembered as Doubting Thomas and was reputed to have travelled to India to spread the gospel there. But the short reference to him in this part of John's gospel seems to throw some light on his character. The disciples didn't want Jesus to go to Judaea, because they were afraid for his life, but Thomas said to them, 'Let us also go, that we may die with him.'

Thomas
I was scared.
We all were,
and I think he was scared too.
We tried to dissuade him from going,
But he had made up his mind
And that was it.
I loved him.
I couldn't bear to think of him going alone,

of him being stoned
or killed outright.
I said to the others,
'Let's go with him.'
So we did.
I loved him,
but I hadn't really grasped
the truth of him,
not until we got there,
not until I saw with my own eyes
Lazarus walking out of his tomb,
alive and free.

These are all things to wonder about and questions to ponder. It may seem futile to ask questions to which there is no definite answer, but asking them helps us to enter into the story, and be caught up in its drama.

When I read and re-read this episode in John's gospel, what strikes me most is not any of the things I have mentioned but the character of Jesus himself. What seems to emerge is the struggle he must have had to reconcile his divinity with his humanity. At one moment he declares to Martha with God-like authority, 'I am the resurrection and the life.' Then only minutes later, when he sees Mary weeping he was 'greatly disturbed in spirit and deeply moved.' Jesus began to weep, and the people standing round said, 'See how he loved him!' Nothing could be more human than this. But moments afterwards he cried with a loud voice, 'Lazarus, come out!' and Jesus, who was God, had performed his greatest miracle.

When I think about this, I begin to understand the great burden Jesus must have carried, and I remember his own words:

Come to me, all you that are weary and are carrying heavy burdens, and I will give you rest. Take my yoke upon you, and learn from me, for I am gentle and humble in heart, and you will find rest for your souls (Matthew 11: 28, 29).

Tuesday in the Fifth Week of Lent
Numbers 21:4-9; John 8:21-30

Today we are taking a day out from concentrating on the scripture readings. We are coming towards the end of Lent, and perhaps it's a good idea to reflect on ourselves for a while.

So far we have dwelt a good deal on sad things and on our own failings, so today it might be refreshing to think more positively. Please count your blessings and make a list of them. You can stop when you get to a hundred!

Now make a written list of what you see to be your strengths. Stop when you get to ten.

Then read through your blessings slowly, giving time to thanking God for each of them.

Go through the same process for your strengths.

You may wonder why I put so much emphasis on this. It is because almost all of us tend to stress the other side of our lives: to bewail our misfortunes and to dwell on our weaknesses and sins. But we don't need to wear sackcloth and ashes. What about garments of praise instead?

The spirit of the Lord is upon me,
because the Lord has anointed me:
he has sent me to bring good news to the oppressed,
to bind up the brokenhearted,
to proclaim liberty to the captives,
and release to the prisoners ...
to provide for those who mourn in Zion –
to give them a garland instead of mourning,
a garment of praise instead of a faint spirit.
Isaiah 61:1,3

Today we are going to look at the letter to the Hebrews. We don't know who wrote this letter, but he gave the Hebrews excellent instructions for how to lead Christian lives which are just as valid for us today. To take a few lines from the letter:

> Let mutual love continue. Do not neglect to show hospitality to strangers, for by doing that some have entertained angels without knowing it. Remember those who are in prison, as though you were in prison with them; those who are being tortured, as though you yourselves are being tortured. Let marriage be held in honour by all ... keep your lives free from the love of money, and be content with what you have; for he has said, 'I will never leave you or forsake you.' So we can say with confidence, 'The Lord is my helper; I will not be afraid. What can anyone do to me?' (Hebrews 13:1-6).

What strikes me most about this advice is the strong emphasis on true compassion, or empathy, in other words getting under the skin of those who are suffering. To the writer of this letter, it is not enough to be concerned for those who are in prison or being tortured; it is not even enough to pray for them. We are to imagine what it is actually like to be them. This confirms what we experience in our ordinary lives, that usually only the bereaved can really help the bereaved, only alcoholics can know what it's like to be an alcoholic. Which doesn't mean, of course, that there is no point in our offering sympathy and comfort, our doing our best to understand what it is really like for those who are trying to reach for our love. But empathy goes beyond concern; it requires perseverance and patience and above all, selflessness.

I think you may find it helpful to study this passage slowly and carefully, and perhaps pick out those nuggets of advice which particularly speak to you. For me, at this time, strangers and those who are in prison are of especial concern to me.

Strangers are often perceived as at threat. People are afraid of them because they are 'other', they are not 'one of us'. And sadly, too often fear leads to hostility and becomes abuse, and strangers, far from being welcomed are shouted and sworn at, bombarded with insults and sometimes bricks.

It seems to some people that our western countries are over-run by strangers: asylum seekers, refugees, immigrant workers, the Roma. We forget – if we ever really knew – that all of these people are our brothers and sisters and have the same needs, the same fears and the same hopes as we do. When we can get over our mistrust and instead welcome and befriend them, then we can start getting to know them. And only at this stage can we begin to empathise with them.

Mention of prison always alerts me because my own son has been to prison and I have visited him there. Although I loved him and wanted to do everything to help him and longed for him to be free, I can't honestly say that it was as though I was in prison with him. How could it be?

Good people, trying to stand in the shoes of the poor or the homeless or any disadvantaged group, sometimes spend a week or longer living as they live. This is a commendable and valiant thing to do, but because it is both temporary and artificial it can't be the same as it is for those whose normal way of life it is.

In a city near where I live there are groups of refugees, some-times called 'Living Ghosts', refugees who, rather than be de-ported to their country of origin which is dangerous for them, choose to stay here without money (their entitlement to any sup-port having been withdrawn when their application to stay had been refused), without food, without a roof over their heads or any chance of work. A local charity gives them five pounds a week and they rely on friends to let them stay in their homes.

Some friends of mine tried to live on five pounds a week and failed spectacularly. They spent money on food only – no clothes, minimal heating, and ran out of cash. They knew they had come nowhere near to being with those strangers as though they were strangers too, but they certainly learnt from their experience.

Thursday in the Fifth Week of Lent
Genesis 17:3-9; John 8:51-59

Today is a day for reflection. During all these weeks little mention of the psalms has been made, but when we read them or listen to them, and meditate slowly on their words, we often find
that their voice is our voice. Although they were written so long
ago, and Jesus himself would have known all of them by heart,
the psalms are ageless, they speak to every generation and every
person.

I have chosen two for your reflection, but today I am not
going to tell you what they mean for me, because I think you
may learn more from your own thought and prayer. It may be a
whole psalm that moves you, or a phrase, or a single word. It
may help you to write your thoughts down.

Psalm 51: A Penitential Psalm
Have mercy on me, O God,
according to your steadfast love;
according to your abundant mercy
blot out my transgressions.
Wash me thoroughly from my iniquity,
and cleanse me from my sin.

For I know my transgressions,
and my sin is ever before me.
Against you, you alone, have I sinned,
And done what is evil in your sight,
so that you are justified in your sentence
and blameless when you pass judgement.
Indeed, I was born guilty,
A sinner when my mother conceived me.

You desire truth in the inward being,
therefore teach me wisdom in my secret heart.
Purge me with hyssop, and I shall be clean,
Wash me, and I shall be whiter than snow.

Let me hear joy and gladness;
let the bones you have crushed rejoice.
Hide your face from my sins
and blot out all my iniquities.

Create in me a clean heart, O God,
and put a new and right spirit within me.
do not cast me away from your presence,
and do not take your Holy Spirit from me.
Restore to me the joy of your salvation
and sustain in me a willing spirit.
…

The sacrifice acceptable to God is a broken spirit,
A broken and contrite heart,
O God, you will not despise.

Psalm 103, selected verses
Bless the Lord my soul
and all that is within me
bless his holy name.
…

The Lord is merciful and gracious,
slow to anger and abounding in steadfast love.
He will not always accuse,
nor will he keep his anger for ever.

He does not deal with us according to our sins,
nor repay us according to our iniquities,
for as the heavens are high above the earth,
so great is his steadfast love
toward those who fear him;
as far as the east is from the west,
so far he removes our transgressions from us.
as a father has compassion for his children,
so the Lord has compassion for those who fear him.

Friday in the Fifth Week of Lent
Jeremiah 20:10-13; John 10:31-42

Today we are going to think again about the kingdom of God. I believe it is not so much a place we can attain by our own efforts, as a state of being which evolves wherever there is goodness and genuine love.

Let us first look at some of the things Jesus had to say about the kingdom of God:

> And do not keep striving for what you are to eat and what you are to drink, and do not keep worrying. For it is the nations of the world that strive after all these things, and your Father knows that you need them. Instead, seek his kingdom, and these things will be given to you as well (Luke 12:29-31).

I guess that most people are like me, in that we do keep worrying about silly things and wasting time thinking about food and drink and what we are to wear instead of seeking the kingdom of God.

> Truly I tell you, the tax collectors and prostitutes are going into the kingdom of God ahead of you (Matthew 21:31)

Why would the tax collectors and prostitutes go into heaven ahead of the chief priests and elders? Maybe because they believed in Jesus, and possibly because they knew themselves to be sincere and were not hypocritical and self-righteous.

> Let the little children come to me, and do not stop them; for it is to such as these that the kingdom of God belongs. Truly I tell you, whoever does not receive the kingdom of God as a little child will not enter it (Luke 18:16).

Why does the kingdom of God belong to little children? Perhaps because of their innocence and openness.

> When Jesus saw that the scribe answered wisely, he said to him, 'You are not far from the kingdom of God.' After that no-one dared to ask him any question (Matthew 12:34)

The scribe was not far from the kingdom of God because he listened to Jesus and learnt from him.

Once Jesus was asked by the Pharisees when the kingdom of God was coming, and he answered, 'The kingdom of God is not coming with things that can be observed; nor will they say, "Look, here it is!" or, "There it is!" For in fact, the kingdom of God is among you (Luke 17:20).

This is the key text about the kingdom of God in the gospels. Some translations read, 'within you' rather than 'among' you. Either way, it is something intangible but the greatest treasure we can seek, already present and active.

The following extract from Isaiah is a metaphor for the Kingdom of God, where peace will reign:

The wolf shall lie down with the lamb,
the leopard shall lie down with the kid,
the calf and the lion and the fatling together,
and a little child shall lead them.
The cow and the bear shall graze,
their young shall graze together;
and the lion shall eat straw like the ox.
The nursing child shall put its hand on the adder's den.
They will not hurt or harm on all my holy mountain;
for the earth will be full of the knowledge of the Lord
as the waters cover the sea.
Isaiah 11:6-9

For personal consideration:
After meditating on this passage from Isaiah, you may like to describe your idea of the kingdom of God, perhaps in writing or poetry, or by painting a picture.

Saturday in the Fifth Week of Lent
Ezekiel 37:21-28; John 11:45-56

We are nearing the end of Lent; tomorrow Holy Week begins.

In the reading from Ezekiel we hear how God is bringing all his people together. He makes a wonderful promise to them, of restoration and reconciliation.

My dwelling place shall be with them; and I will be their God, and they shall be my people.

Taking this journey through Lent, we have listened to God's word and reflected on him and on ourselves. But the journey is not exclusively about God and me, it is about me as just one of God's children. Because to live our lives to the full, to be whole and holy, we have to remember that God's vision is for the whole of humanity. We are his people and he is our God.

John also had a vision:

Then one of the elders addressed me, saying, 'Who are these, robed in white, and where do they come from?' I said to him, 'Sir, you are the one that knows.' Then he said to me, 'These are they who have come out of the great ordeal; they have washed their robes and made them white in the blood of the Lamb.

For this reason they are before the throne of God,

and worship him day and night within his temple,

and the one who is seated on the throne will shelter them.

They will hunger no more, and thirst no more;

the sun will not strike them, nor any scorching heat;

for the Lamb at the centre of the throne will be their shepherd,

and he will guide them to the springs of the water of life,

and God will wipe away every tear from their eyes.

Revelation 7:15-17

Your future, our future, may bring consolation, may be a challenge, or both.

Tomorrow we begin Holy Week and try to immerse ourselves in reflecting on the last days on earth of our Lord Jesus Christ, God and man, before he met his death.

For personal thought or group discussion:
We can't know how near the truth John's vision was. What, if anything, appeals to you about it?
Do you have a vision of your own concerning the 'after-life'?

Passion Sunday
Luke 19:28-40; Isaiah 50:4-7; Philippians 2:6-11; Luke 22:14-23:56

For a child, Passion Sunday can be something special, something to look forward to because it's different from the usual Sunday. There are funny little crosses to carry and a grand procession outside. But adults who have been doing this for many years, can be quite grumpy. Some will complain that the crosses are poorly made: they come undone as soon as you look at them. Some are reluctant to get on their feet and leave their warm comfortable seat to go out to where, like as not, it's rainy and cold. Still others get quite cross about the singing, and it does seem inevitable that by the end, the front of the procession will be singing a completely different line from those at the back.

But if we pause to think, we will have a quite different attitude. We will realise that it was probably a long trying job for whoever struggled to make the hundreds of palms neat and cross-like. We will understand that it's good to be remembering the first Palm Sunday, and to be all together singing in praise of God and being witnesses of our faith to passers-by.

More importantly, if we start to remember what happened to Jesus and is commemorated on this day, we will feel sad, not because of our own discomfort or irritations, but for him. There is something specially tragic about this gospel incident. The friends of Jesus, and the crowds along the way, were all so happy, so full of praise and love for the young man on the donkey. We know, as they couldn't know, that in less than a week all but a few friends would have deserted him and the crowds would be full of hate and baying for his death.

Great joy suddenly turned into profound sorrow. How poignant, then, is this day when Jesus knew himself to be the focus of love and adoration and what must have seemed to be loyal commitment. In our prayers we so often ask Jesus to have pity on us, to comfort us. On this Passion Sunday it is our turn to feel compassion for him, to long somehow to prevent what is going to happen to him.

The hymns we associate with Palm Sunday, as this day used to be called, are triumphant ones, such as: 'Hail, Redeemer, King Divine' and 'Ride on, ride on, in majesty', but I wonder, is that really how we think of Jesus riding on his donkey? Of course we have no idea what Jesus looked like, in spite of wonderful paintings that have tried to depict him, but there is a word picture written by St Paul which is one of the most moving pieces of poetry in the bible, and which seems to describe the essential Jesus, whether riding on a donkey or hanging from a cross. The church uses this poem, from Paul's letter to the Philippians, on this day as the second reading of the Mass.

His state was divine,
yet Christ Jesus did not cling
to his equality with God
but emptied himself
to assume the condition of a slave,
and became as men are,
and being as all men are,
he was humbler yet,
even to accepting death,
death on a cross.
But God raised him high
and gave him the name
which is above all other names
so that all beings
in the heavens and in the underworld,
should bend the knee at the name of Jesus
and every tongue should acclaim
Jesus Christ as Lord,
to the glory of the Father.
Philippians 2:6-11

What can we learn for ourselves from today? Perhaps to appreciate the virtue of humility. Immediately before the meditation from Philippians that we have just read, Paul says, 'Let the same mind be in you that was in Christ Jesus.' Of course Paul is asking too much. How can any of us aspire to have the same mind as

Jesus? Yet perhaps we can school ourselves to become more aware of our shortcomings and weaknesses in regard to humility. Jesus was never a doormat, allowing people to 'walk over' him, nor would he want us to be. He was never proud or overbearing, nor was he falsely humble as so often we are tempted to be. Time and time again we shrug off compliments although we know them to be true. It is not humble to cringe away from responsibility; humility requires us to be candid and courageous.

It is worthwhile to sit with the gospel narrative which today is taken from St Luke, on our own, perhaps at home before or after Mass. When we read scripture, we are all struck by different words, stories, or phrases. I will draw out some of today's gospel that I feel particularly appealing or instructive, in the hope that readers will be encouraged to find their own inspiration.

At the beginning of the narrative, the disciples are with Jesus, about to eat the Passover meal. He says he is longing to eat this Passover with them. It isn't often in the gospels that Christ's humanity comes to the fore, and here it is touching to see his eager desire to be with his friends to enjoy a last meal with them.

After the meal there is a marked change in Luke's account of the passion. We begin to have a hint of the depth of Christ's suffering. In the Garden of Gethsemane he again shows the weakness of his humanity, begging his friends to stay with him. As his prayer grows more intense, his sweat becomes like great drops of blood falling on the ground. Contemplating this scene is like being able to do nothing but stand by when someone is in the throes of anguish. We long to comfort them, to put our arms round them, to find the right words, but all we can give them is silence and gentle presence. Although it happened so long ago, it makes us feel helpless.

It is impossible to know what made Jesus suffer most: was it the physical pain: the flogging, the crown of thorns, the falls on the way to Calvary, the nails tearing flesh and bone, the stretch of his body on the cross? Or was it the humiliation, the mocking, the jeers of the soldiers and the crowds, the desertion of his friends? I believe it was all of these, and that his awareness of the anguish felt by his mother and those faithful ones who loved him was for him the cruellest of all his suffering.

In Luke's account of the passion, which we have read or heard today, there are many incidents and exchanges for us to reflect on. I have chosen on this day to focus on the stories of Simon of Cyrene and the Women of Jerusalem. We know scarcely anything about Simon. Was he annoyed or pleased or frightened to be ordered to help Jesus? Did he change after walking the road to Calvary with him?

Simon of Cyrene
I was annoyed when they picked me
and those soldiers dragged me forward.
I can't help it if I stand out; people always notice me.
I'm blacker than all these Jews.
Anyway, there I was,
big black Simon minding his own business
when they grabbed me none too gently
and one of them said,
'You've got to carry his cross.'
I didn't know what he was talking about,
I'm new to Jerusalem.
I'd just come to see what all the noise was about,
and was standing at the edge of the crowd
when they pushed me towards him.
I looked down at him there on the ground
He just seemed – well, the word is 'sad',
and although he was bloody and filthy
he seemed to have a strange dignity.
The soldiers prodded me roughly,
told me to get on with the job,
so I bent right down to his level
and with his face so close to mine,
a face smeared with sweat and tears and blood,
I felt suddenly happy
and proud to be carrying that cross
for someone, who, whatever he was,

was certainly no criminal.

I thought he might be someone I could truly love.

It is thought that the 'women of Jerusalem' may have been some of those who had supported Jesus during his ministry. We also know that noble women of the city used to give sedative drinks to men who were condemned to die. It is interesting that Jesus spoke so clearly to these women. By this time he must have been scarcely able to think, let alone speak.

Daughters of Jerusalem

We made ourselves walk alongside him, although it was almost more than we could bear to see him treated as a common criminal, staggering under that heavy cross with blood running down his face.

This was Jesus, who knew us and loved us. Some of us women had been following the crowds for years, listening to his teaching, marvelling at his miraculous healings. Others of us had brought food for him and his disciples, and washed and mended their clothes. And only five days ago we were so happy, cheering as he came into Jerusalem, riding on a donkey. I shouted till I was hoarse.

But now we were all silent, all weeping. Suddenly he lifted his face and looked straight us. Even in his pain and fear and degradation, his eyes were full of compassion and he spoke directly to us saying,

'Daughters of Jerusalem, do not weep for me; weep rather for yourselves and your children.'

That was just like him.

It never ceases to amaze us, that after so much suffering, Jesus was willing to forgive those who crucified him.

In Luke's account, just before he died, Jesus said, 'Father, into your hands I commend my spirit.' He breathed his last, confident of God's welcoming love.

For personal thought or group discussion:
1. Is there one thing which has touched you more than any other during this day?
2. What things stand out for you in Luke's account of the passion?

It would be a pity to end this day agitated and exhausted by trying to take in so much. Perhaps you would like to end by sitting quietly with a lighted candle, and for a short while meditating on just one thing that has meant something for you today.

Monday in Holy Week
Isaiah 42:1-7; John 12: 1-11

Today, at weekday Mass, the gospel is taken from John, and is an account of what happened only six days before the Passover meal which was the start of Christ's passion, his dreadful journey towards death.

Here is a picture of Jesus with his friends: Lazarus, for whom he wept, Martha, the worrier, and Mary who seems to have been a deeply spiritual woman blessed with special insight. It was not easy for Martha to understand her sister.

I think most of us find it easier to identify with Martha, rather than her extraordinary sister. But then most of us are happier blending in with the crowd, being the same as everyone else than we would be if called to stand up and be counted. Nor would we like to take an extravagant initiative like Mary's, bound to be unpopular. From the first time we met them in the gospels, the sisters are shown to have contrasting characteristics, and they have come to represent in our minds contemplation (Mary) and action (Martha).

Martha
Mary is so different from me.
I like to do; she likes to be.
She is the quiet one
unobtrusive, shy in company.
So you can guess how surprised I was,
shocked, actually,
when she came into that room full of people
carrying the precious jar
of costly perfume.
Everyone was looking,
and all of us stared in astonishment,
as Mary tipped the whole jar of sweet-smelling nard
over the feet of Jesus.

Nobody said anything,
nobody moved
as my sister knelt
and dried his feet with her loosened hair.
Then Judas spoke,
(I never liked him much)
criticising the waste.
But Jesus spoke up for Mary.
'Leave her alone,' he said.
'She bought it so that she might keep it
for the day of my burial.'
When he said this,
there was a gasp in the room.
Peter said something like
'No! That's nonsense, Lord,
you'll live to a good old age.'
But seeing Mary's face,
I understood the truth
and burst into floods of tears.
I just couldn't help it.
…

Mary
I don't know why I did it,
but suddenly I was sure it was the right thing to do.
I knew people wouldn't like it
and Martha wouldn't understand,
but the only important thing to me then
was to show him he was loved, really loved.

I knew him so well now
I could tell that deep inside he was afraid
and sensed that something terrible would happen to him soon
I know I seem different,
different from my comforting, comfortable sister,
but we are alike in what matters most to both of us:
our love for the Son of God.

Some people, like the Poor Clares and the Carmelites, dedicate their whole lives to prayers; others are so immersed in doing good works for God's Kingdom that they forget about him altogether and neglect to pray. It seems likely that most, if not all of us, have both a Mary and a Martha in us, and perhaps it is unwise for those who are not called to a special vocation, to cultivate one at the expense of the other, because God needs us for both action and prayer.

We may like to pause for a while and think about this. Am I a Martha or a Mary? Do I need to change so that my life becomes more balanced and more pleasing to God?

For personal thought and group discussion:
1. Which are you more like, Martha or Mary?
2. Which comes more easily to you, prayer or Christian action?

Tuesday in Holy Week
Isaiah 49:1-6; John 13:21-33, 36-38

Simon Peter is one of the most endearing characters in the gospels. We can imagine the other disciples pretending, from sheer embarrassment, that he was nothing to do with them. We can also imagine that his antics often made them laugh, as when he leapt into the sea of Galilee determined to walk on the water, like Jesus, and almost immediately started to sink. Life would never be dull with Peter around.

Yesterday, we were thinking about Martha and Mary. Martha, too, must have been embarrassed by her sister's behaviour, but Mary was a very different character from Peter. He certainly does not seem to have been a quiet, contemplative person, nor was Mary noted for being funny or tactless or attention-seeking! Personalities were complex then as they are today.

I have said that I think that most of us, perhaps especially women, identify easily with Martha. I also believe that most of us, women and men, see ourselves as having many of Peter's traits. Peter was bold, rash, impetuous, bungling, clumsy, insensitive, noisy, foolish, extrovert. He acted before he thought. But Peter's redeeming feature was that he was so human. He didn't do things by halves. He was certainly a fool at times, but capable of great remorse.

We may wonder why Jesus chose such a man to lead his church. I suggest it was because he was eminently lovable. Also he was willing to change, and he did change.

Peter
God knows
I've done so many stupid things in my life,
but today I've hit the bottom, the pits.
They all saw me blubbering, just now,
the maid and that servant of the High Priest.
They'll be laughing at me for crying like a baby,
but I deserve it.
I don't care what people think of me any more.

I was so full of myself.
(I always am, that's half the trouble)
always shouting the odds.
And I made that foolish boast,
they all heard me –
'Lord, I will be ready to go to prison with you,
and to death!'
Only I let him down.
The great show-off, Simon Peter,
a pathetic coward and a liar.
But what about him?
I've let him down so badly,
and if they condemn him,
and, God forbid, he dies,
Jesus, the best man that ever walked this earth,
I'll never know
if he could have forgiven me.

For personal thought and group discussion:
1. Do you believe that people can change for the better?
2. What do you like most about Peter?

Wednesday in Holy Week
Isaiah 50:4-9; Matthew 26:14-25

In today's gospel we hear about Judas Iscariot and his plan to betray Jesus. The day used to be known among Catholics as Spy Wednesday, and Judas was almost universally hated and despised among Christians. His name has entered our language to mean 'traitor'.

Attitudes are, however, slowly changing. In the first place, those who sincerely want to be Christ-like don't hold on to feelings of hatred, particularly when, as in the case of Judas, he showed such bitter remorse. Secondly, there is a way of understanding scripture which suggests that Judas did not have freedom to choose the way he behaved towards Jesus, that he betrayed the person who meant most to him 'in order that the scriptures might be fulfilled'. But thirdly, and most importantly, I believe that suicides deserve compassion.

During my lifetime, the way we think about people who take their own lives has changed dramatically. At one time suicide was condemned as the worst sin, the fruit of despair, and suicides were denied burial in holy ground. In some parts of the country they were buried at a crossroads with a stake through the heart! Even quite recently I have heard people denounce a son for his disregard of his mother's feelings in ending his life. It seems to me that nobody would kill themselves unless they were reduced to the blackest despair, a state in which they are incapable of making moral judgements. To be suffering enough to want – and need – to kill oneself is surely enough punishment for anyone. So I would argue that compassion towards a suicide is a more appropriate sentiment than hate or condemnation.

Like most people I have been deeply moved and troubled by the suicide of someone dear to me. The one which was most distressing, because I loved her and because she must have suffered such anguish, was the death of a bright and beautiful young girl who drowned herself in a lake. How could anyone think of blaming her? And Judas?

Judas

No-one understands me:
Sometimes something forces me to do things,
to go against his teaching,
to act without love.
Afterwards I hate myself.
I'm not normal like the others.
I know I am an oddity,
and sometimes it's as though
I'm programmed to do bad things.
Even so, I never dreamt that I
could be so wicked, so full of sin, so evil
as to betray the only one who loved me,
the only one I loved: Jesus.

I was greedy for the money, of course.
I had always been poor
and I had never owned
thirty pieces of silver.
It seemed beautiful to me then,
that blood money.
But worse than the money was the kiss,
hideous, horrible hypocrisy!
How could he bear it so calmly,
looking at me with pity?

I hadn't given any thought
to what would happen.
I watched and listened steathily,
the horror grew
and I was powerless to stop it,
I who had set it all in motion.

When I saw him hanging there,
my Jesus, nailed to a cross
I cried to the Father,
'Let us change places.
Let him come down

and nail me there to die.'
But nothing happened.

I knew I was only fit for hell,
beyond forgiveness,
worth absolutely nothing.
It was time to end my useless life
my pitiful existence.
So I took a rope
and went to find a tree.

For personal thought or group discussion:
What are your thoughts on a) suicide, b) Judas?

Holy Thursday
Exodus 12:1-8, 11-14; Corinthians 11:23-26; John 13: 1-15

This is a very busy day in the life of the church. At the Chrism Mass, in the morning, the priests of the diocese gather with the bishop. The holy oils are blessed and the priests take them back to their parishes where they will be used in the sacraments of baptism, confirmation, ordination and the anointing of the sick to give healing and strength to the people.

In the evening, we celebrate the Mass of the Lord's Supper, remembering Christ's twofold giving of himself. Representing Jesus, the priest kneels to wash the feet of his people. At one time it was usually a few hand-picked servers who were chosen for this privilege; now, at least in some churches, it is volunteers, women as well as men, who can have their feet washed, a humbling experience. As at every Mass, the priest reflects the words of Christ, saying, 'This is my body ... this is my blood' and the whole emphasis of the service is on the self-giving love which we are called to imitate.

I like to meditate on the scene of Jesus washing the feet of his disciples. For me, the way he showed such humility and tenderness towards his friends is a powerful expression of his giving himself to us in love that is easier to grasp and to cope with than the crucifixion itself, which is of course the supreme act of self-giving love.

The washing of the feet is not horrifying and terrifying like the suffering and death on the cross (on which of course I will also reflect). Although such a surprising thing, to the disciples, for Jesus to do, the setting is nonetheless homely, the scene domestic.

Peter, as so often, succeeds in making himself the centre of attention, but sometimes I think about those men, his close friends. I wonder what they thought about the exchange between Jesus and Peter. I wonder about the disciples of whom we know little more than their name, James the Less, for instance.

James the Less
I always like to be with the Master
on formal occasions like that.
Normally, with Jesus,
everything's informal,
but not this Passover.
We were all wearing clean clothes,
the lamb smelt wonderful,
we were warm and comfortable,
and, for once, indoors
in a decent room,
for once, just Jesus
and us and close friends,
the women who prepared the food for us
somewhere in the background.
I was happy,
I think we all were,
though looking back,
Judas must have been pretty tense,
and of course Jesus must have been weighed down
by his hidden sorrow.
So what happened was all the more surprising.
I just couldn't believe it.
We were all enjoying the meal
when suddenly Jesus stood up.
He said nothing,
but took off his outer garment,
wrapped a towel round his waist,
poured water into a basin
and began to wash our feet!
We were astonished, silent,
watching and waiting our turn
until he came to Peter.

I admire Peter, I wish I was more like him,
but I didn't like the way
he argued with the Master.

He was flushed and angry and he shouted.
It didn't seem reasonable to me.
After all, Jesus knows what is right.

I was the last.
Jesus rose from his knees.
He changed the water.
It was clean, for me!
When he tested it with his finger
In case it was too hot or too cold,
I felt tears running.
This – for me?
To give himself with such humility,
such tenderness,
to me, James the Less!

You may wish to meditate on the washing of feet from a different viewpoint. On Holy Thursday, after Communion, the Blessed Sacrament is taken from the tabernacle and carried in reverent procession, to another place. The tabernacle is now empty, but many people stay in church, to adore the Sacrament in the small chapel or other place where it has been placed.

I lived for four years in an ecumenical community where Christians of many different traditions worked and relaxed and prayed together. One of the members was a little nun with a huge imagination and lots of artistic skill called Julian, and she made wonderful contributions to our Triduum. We were very privileged in having on our premises not only an ancient, beautiful church just outside the east wing of the house, but within the same house, a small oratory, built in Tudor times.

It was one of Julian's tasks to decorate this chapel, with its Altar of Repose, on the night before the crucifixion in readiness for the Good Friday Vigil. She began weeks beforehand, collecting branches from the gardens and bringing them indoors where she tried to find just the place and temperature for the buds to open at the right time. After the solemn service on Holy Thursday, the priest would reverently carry the Blessed

Sacrament to the oratory chapel and place it in the tabernacle there. On that night, the chapel was a touching and lovely sight. I seem to remember it brought tears to my eyes. To welcome Our Lord, Julian had filled the chapel with sweetly-smelling flowers and newly-opened buds. No part of that house ever looked as beautiful as on that holy night. It was Julian's sorrowing welcome, on behalf of us all, to our sorrowing Lord.

For personal thought or group discussion:
1. Can you imagine Jesus washing your feet?
3. What appeals to you most about Holy Thursday?

Good Friday
Isaiah 52:13-53:12; Hebrews 4:14-16, 5:7-9; John 18:1-19:42

There is a great deal to meditate on today. In church, we listen again to the gospel description of the passion, this time attributed to John. We also venerate the cross, and intercede for the world and its peoples.

Alone, we may choose to reflect on one incident or one character in the story. I have chosen someone without a name, who is very significant for me: the Repentant Thief. Of the gospel writers, only Luke mentions him, only Luke tells his story, and perhaps this in itself makes what happened even more poignant. Luke's account reminds us of the danger of condemning all criminals as beyond redemption or as people we 'don't want to know'.

There is a story behind every crime, and a history to every criminal. It is when we understand that criminals are complex human beings just like anyone else that we can begin to adopt a less judgemental punitive attitude towards them. The men and women who are given long prison sentences are not necessarily more wicked than you or me. It is certainly possible that some of them are more generous, braver, more compassionate than I am. I believe we need to get away from the idea of lumping together all those who are guilty of a crime and locking them up in institutions.

The Repentant Thief
I think I had always expected it: the cross,
my father and two of my uncles had died that way after all,
and I was as bad as any of them, worse perhaps.
I could say I never had a chance.
My mother, who was beautiful warm and loving,
but a bad lot too in her way I suppose,
stoned to death by angry men.
I grew up with robbers. It was the way we all lived,
always hungry; always filthy,

always angry with the rich, with life, with God.
But to be honest I knew all along
that there was something better,
that there was a better way to live.
It may have been the memory of my mother's tenderness,
an old man I had once seen praying fervently,
the unexpected sight of wild flowers, bright and lovely,
or words overheard as I sneaked by the Temple.
It may have been all of these things
and others now forgotten,
but I cannot bring myself to pretend,
pretend I was simply the victim of circumstance,
that I never had a chance
or any choice,
that I couldn't help being a thief,
a man of violence,
a man without love.
Where tenderness, beauty and the name of God,
glimpses of light in my muddled world,
had touched me but failed to move me,
I was moved at last
when I saw him, Jesus, hanging near me on his cross.

His body was already half broken,
his face tortured, wet with blood and sweat and tears,
his eyes staring with pain, his mouth taut in agony.
The thief on the other side of him jeered,
and then, for the last time, in these last moments of my life,
I broke free.
I felt anger, as usual,
and, as never before, love.
I spoke. I don't know what I said,
scolding the other fellow,
but looking at Jesus and feeling for him.
for the first time in my life I forgot myself.

He lifted his head and looked into my eyes.
In that moment I felt no pain from the cruel drag of the nails,
no fear, not even shame.
I felt empty, and then slowly filled
with light and warmth and love as he looked at me.
He could not smile, his voice was cracked and hoarse,
but his words and his meaning were unmistakable.
To me, the most miserable of sinners, he said,
'Today you will be with me in paradise,'
and then I knew joy.

* * *

It was Good Friday. Teresa was in church, standing in the long line of people waiting to venerate the cross. It was a large crucifix, placed on a stool at the bottom of the sanctuary steps, and steadied by two young servers. Hundreds of people silently processed to kneel (as far as they were able) and kiss the feet of the figure of Jesus.

Teresa had taken part in this ritual for as long as she could remember. She had received comments on it from friends of different traditions or none, who could not believe she would take part in something so (the adjectives varied according to the personality of the accuser) demeaning, primitive, atavistic, medieval, humiliating, unreal. But Teresa found that this solemn gesture encapsulated what she felt and thought about Christ crucified. To her it seemed perfectly appropriate to kneel and kiss the feet of 'Jesus', and be just one among the hundreds doing the same. For her it was not humiliating; it was expressing the utter humility she felt before this crucifix and all it represented.

She was only sixth in line from the cross when to her horror her mobile phone rang, piercing the reverent silence. In a panic, she pulled it from her pocket and was on the point of switching it off when the name of the sender caught her eye. Eileen. Teresa switched off the phone, left the queue (by now she was third in line) and hurried out to the porch. Eileen was a very close friend. Why on earth was she phoning now? She had said she would be in her church at this time. There must be an emergency ... Teresa punched Eileen's number and the ring was answered at once. But she could only hear sobbing and a sort of raw moaning. 'Eileen, whatever is it?' she said, 'Tell me!' But Eileen could only manage two words: 'Come, please!'

It was only half a mile to Eileen's house. Teresa ran all the way and arrived breathless. She stepped through the open door and stopped. In front of her on the bottom step of the stairs sat Eileen, cradling the lifeless body of her teenage son, Miles, on her lap. His neck was badly bruised and swollen; his face was unrecognisable. 'I found him hanging,' whispered Eileen.

As Teresa stood for a second, immobile with shock, another scene flashed into her mind: the intensely moving carving by Michaelangelo, known as the Pieta, showing Mary cradling her crucified son on her lap. Then she began the tasks of a good friend.

Sometimes we try to separate the holy and the human. Yet when Teresa stood waiting to kneel at the feet of Jesus in church, she was the same person as the woman who rushed from the ceremony of that solemn ritual to attend to her friend with heartfelt compassion. The suffering of Jesus and the suffering of Miles were very different, and yet united in the presence of God and the awakening of love.

For personal thought or group discussion:
1. What part of the ceremonies on Good Friday move you most?
2. Which incident in the passion of Jesus moves you most?
3. How is the story of Teresa relevant to this day?

Holy Saturday

This is a 'nothing' day, isn't it? There is silence, emptiness, waiting, growing anticipation. Jesus is dead. He has gone from the tabernacle in our churches: the focus of our worship is no longer there.

On this day some people choose to confess their sins, others (or perhaps the same ones) fall hungrily, after a long and faithful time of fasting, on hot cross buns. If possible I like to make this in-between day a quiet, thoughtful time, looking back on how I have spent my Lent, not letting myself look forward just yet.

It's a day when I prefer to be alone, when I like my surroundings simple, plain and bare to reflect the mood of Holy Saturday:
nothing
silence
emptiness
waiting
still
a pale gray day
after yesterday's black
and the shining gold of tomorrow.

This is a day when I prefer to be alone, but life goes on. Saturday, holy or not, the time for shopping and baking and cleaning the house, cleaning the car, cutting the grass ... Saturday, the time for children, the baby, the teenagers, a day for grandmother or the old man next door. Saturday, a friend coming round unexpectedly, needing a shoulder to cry on. Saturday, and there is noise: family noise, the radio with news of disaster, the CD player, belting out rap, then Bach, then rap ... But in the end, in the evening early, I find my own time and space where I can be alone.

I think about this Lent, these past six weeks. I remember my failures, my mistakes and weaknesses. I remember the journey of Jesus and his suffering, too dreadful to imagine. I remember the incidents that have moved me particularly; the times I felt humbled and the times I felt encouraged. I choose one or two readings to read and reflect on. And gradually, I realise that I have felt closer to Our Lord as the weeks slid by. I re-live moments of peace, moments of illumination. I am filled with thankfulness, and hope and increased self-awareness. And I can't help wondering, if I had been there, would I have dared to stand with Mary and John at the foot of the cross?

Were you there when they crucified the Lord?
Were you there when they crucified the Lord?
Yes. I was there, standing at the very edge of the crowd,
Pretending to be pausing on the way to somewhere else,
But in reality riveted
To what was happening to Jesus and those with him.
I saw Veronica's impetuous dash
to wipe the sweat from his face,
And even as I condemned her action
For its display and lack of control and sheer futility –
I wished it could have been me.
I drew nearer then.
I saw the way he looked.
I saw his pain and humiliation
And saw – could it have been fear?
I saw his shattered body
Grotesquely hoisted without dignity
I heard him cry out,
I heard the desperation in his voice.
And for a moment I was moved to join
The crowd of mourners at his feet,
His mother, his friends and other nameless people.
But I suppressed my impulse; I walked away.
Like the rich young man I grieved,
Unable to commit myself to him.
That much courage, that much love,
I could not give.

Father, forgive me, for I knew what I was doing.

I was there when they crucified the Lord.

I begin to wonder about Jesus on this day. Where is he? Where was he on the first Holy Saturday? Does he lie, tightly wrapped in swaddling clothes as he was all those years ago in the manger at Bethlehem? Does he lie, imprisoned in that stone-cold tomb, unmoving like any corpse?

Or does he, as the old legends have it, secretly spring forth from his grave on this day and descend into hell? That is what people believed in medieval times. Hell is painted as a great dragon, the colour of blood, its enormous mouth wide open to show all the writhing bodies of those who died since the beginning of the world. Jesus stands at the entrance to this cavernous mouth, waiting to welcome those who come stumbling forth into his light, his forgiving embrace.

We see that Adam and Eve are stepping out, incredulous in their joy, and as I think on this scene I feel sure my mind's eye sees the timid figure of Judas, poised on the threshold, hardly daring to lift his eyes to Jesus who is beckoning him with a smile. I remember how we used to recite in the old creed: 'He descended into hell, and on the third day he rose again.' So Jesus, we might assume, went back into his grave, waiting, as we are, for tomorrow.

Later that same evening, we are all gathered in the church. We stand in darkness, waiting, each with an unlit candle in his or her hand. Suddenly, at the back of the church, something shines, and the priest comes in lifting the Paschal Candle high in his hands. Then, gradually, we light one another's candles till the whole church is beautiful with light, and we are ready now together, ready for the completion of our pilgrimage, the fulfilment of our Lent, ready to meet and greet our Risen Lord.

Endpiece

O Lord, I am a pilgrim,
I have walked the way with you.
You watched over me as a shepherd watches over his flock,
your right hand held me fast.
Truly, goodness and mercy have followed me
all the days of my journey.
Yes, I have stumbled more than once
as you stumbled on the way to Calvary.
Yes, I have doubted, when the going got tough,
but I heard you calling.
I was downcast and distressed,
but you heal the broken-hearted.
Though I walked through the valley of the shadow,
you were there, you consoled me.
I drank from your living water
and I was filled with joy,
but I strayed from the path
and fell into the pit.
You rescued me, you embraced me,
you prepared a feast for me
and invited me to your banquet.
You led me the way I should go,
you showed me the dispossessed,
the poor and the lame and the hungry,
and you gave a light to those
who dwell in the land of darkness.
You have sent me forth to be
mother to the motherless,
a sister among sisters,
a daughter of God.
Lord, be my refuge and my strength.